Opera

100 ESSENTIAL CDs

THE ROUGH GUIDE

⌐ **W9-CLO-599**

There are more than one hundred and fifty Rough Guide
travel, phrasebook, and music titles, covering destinations
from Amsterdam to Zimbabwe, languages from Czech to
Thai, and musics from World to Opera and Jazz

Other 100 Essential CD titles

Classical Music • Reggae • Rock

Rough Guides on the Internet

www.roughguides.com

Rough Guide Credits

Text editor: Jonathan Buckley
Series editor: Mark Ellingham
Typesetting: Katie Pringle

Publishing Information

This first edition published September 1999 by
Rough Guides Ltd, 62–70 Shorts Gardens, London, WC2H 9AB

Distributed by the Penguin Group:
Penguin Books Ltd, 27 Wrights Lane, London W8 5TZ
Penguin Books USA Inc., 375 Hudson Street, New York 10014, USA
Penguin Books Australia Ltd, 487 Maroondah Highway,
PO Box 257, Ringwood, Victoria 3134, Australia
Penguin Books Canada Ltd, 10 Alcorn Avenue,
Toronto, Ontario, Canada M4V 1E4
Penguin Books (NZ) Ltd, 182–190 Wairau Road,
Auckland 10, New Zealand

Typeset in Bembo and Helvetica to an original design by Henry Iles.
Printed in Spain by Graphy Cems.

A catalogue record for this book is available from the British Library.
ISBN 1-85828-451-1

Opera

100 ESSENTIAL CDs

THE ROUGH GUIDE

by Matthew Boyden

Contents

Introduction

There has never been a better time to explore opera, now that almost every significant example of the genre can be heard on CD. The choice can be daunting, however. Giuseppe Verdi, for example, completed more than thirty operas, of which there are more than two hundred studio recordings in the catalogue. Add to this tally the plethora of live recordings that are stocked by specialist shops, and you begin to see how unguided exploration can easily lead to expensive disappointment. The **Rough Guide to 100 Essential Opera CDs** gives you a map through this maze of material.

This book does not purport to be a selection of the "best" 100 operas – any such list would be too subjective to be useful. Instead, it discusses 100 key works by the seminal figures (arranged as an A to Z by composer, with works arranged chronologically within each composer entry), ranging from Claudio Monteverdi's *Orfeo*, the earliest opera to have survived in the mainstream repertoire, to Harrison Birtwistle's *Gawain*, one of the major creations of the 1990s. When recommending our first-choice CDs we've generally given preference to recent recordings, but in several instances there are mono or early stereo sets that are so superior as performances that they demand inclusion. Don't assume, though, that the sound quality on any of these older sets is going to impair your enjoyment of the music – modern remastering techniques can make so-called "historic" recordings sound remarkably fresh. If you want to explore the ever-expanding roster of archival recordings, or get a more comprehensive overview of the repertoire, then you should move on to *The Rough Guide to Opera*, the definitive one-volume book on the subject.

All our recommended recordings are available in both Europe and North America, although some may require a special order – no store will have all these discs in stock at any one time. Every review is illustrated with the cover of the current edition, but bear in mind that classical music is re-packaged and re-released so frequently that some of our recommendations will certainly re-emerge in different form before too long. So if the catalogue shows that the recording you want is no longer around, get your stockist to check if the same performance has re-emerged with a new catalogue number – it's extremely unlikely that any of the CDs in this book will ever become extinct. Reissues are quite often sold at a lower price than the original release, but sometimes they come with a booklet synopsis rather than a full libretto. The great majority of the sets we've chosen do have a libretto included; the few exceptions are clearly identified.

Opera is a subject as rich as the novel, encompassing an extraordinary variety of work: the courtly extravaganzas of Lully; the acerbic satires of Kurt Weill; Richard Wagner's garguantuan philosophical mythologies; the witty frivolities of Offenbach; the thrilling vocal pyrotechnics of Donizetti. Here you'll find the whole world of opera condensed into just 200 pages. Whatever your tastes, there are recordings in this book that you'll want to listen to over and over again.

Acknowledgements

The author would like to express his gratitude to all those at the record companies who have provided their assistance in the completion of this book. Thanks also to Anne Hegerty for proofreading and to Katie Pringle for typesetting. And many thanks, as ever, to Jonathan Buckley and Lorraine Bradshaw (the mother of all invention).

Matthew Boyden

John Adams

Nixon in China

Sanford Sylvan (Chou En-Lai), James Maddalena (Richard Nixon), Thomas Hammons (Henry Kissinger), John Duykers (Mao Tse-Tung), Carolann Page (Pat Nixon), Trudy Ellen Craney (Madame Mao); Orchestra of St Luke's; Edo De Waart (conductor)

Nonesuch 7559-79177–2; 2 CDs; full price

It is surprising – shocking, even – how few contemporary composers have opted to make operas out of the material of the modern world. One who has is John Adams, who once remarked that "the myths of our time are not Cupid and Psyche but characters like Mao and Nixon". Adams' faith in opera's contemporary vitality is reflected in his major stage works, *Nixon in China*, *The Death of Klinghoffer* (set aboard the hijacked liner Achille Lauro) and his recent *I Was Looking at the Ceiling and Then I Saw the Sky* (set in Los Angeles during an earthquake). *Nixon in China* showed just how powerfully contemporary events could be turned into opera, earning itself a large and appreciative audience – something most opera composers of the last half-century have had to do without.

Nixon in China reflects on the groundbreaking visit to China, in February 1972, by President Nixon, his wife and Henry Kissinger – a subject proposed to Adams by the director Peter Sellars, who has collaborated with the composer on all his stage works. Nixon is introduced to Chairman Mao, and finds his ideas obscure, but a banquet produces a rapprochement. Pat Nixon is taken on a sight-seeing tour and later joins her husband and Chairman and Madame Mao at a performance of the revolutionary ballet *The Red Detachment of Women*, in which Kissinger somehow becomes involved. On the Americans' last night in Peking each of the opera's main characters considers the events they have witnessed, and what they mean. The last words falls to Chou En-Lai, who wonders, "How much of what we did was good?"

Reviewing *Nixon*, the critic from the New York Times remarked, "Mr Adams has done for the arpeggio what McDonald's did for the hamburger." It's a good line, but it ignores the opera's real achievements in finding striking orchestral colours to dramatize what might easily have been simply garish. Sections of *Nixon* display the same sort of highly kinetic repetitive rhythms as you'll hear in Philip Glass (see p.59), but it shows the dramatic potential of a style that combines Minimalist procedures with more dramatic forms of writing. There is humour in Adams' score, as there is in the libretto, but there is also a real poignancy, as in Nixon's Act I aria "News has a kind of mystery", which expresses an innocent wonderment at the enormity of the events in which he is participating. It is typical of Adams' subtle delineation of his characters that here "mystery" rhymes (several lines later) with "history" as Tricky Dicky muses, "Though we spoke quietly, the eyes and ears of history caught every gesture". Undoubtedly the Nixons have their doltish moments (this opera is by no means a whitewash), but they are not mere caricatures.

Musically, Adams reveals a virtuoso command of stylistic allusion, partly as a means to fuel his melodic imagination, but also to serve a dramatic purpose. Madame Mao's entrance aria brings to mind Mozart's stratospheric aria for the Queen of the Night in *Die Zauberflöte*. Like Mozart's Queen, Madame Mao is an enigma, at once a supernatural being and a creature of flesh and blood, and the allusion concisely encapsulates her dual nature. If occasionally Adams' word-setting is undistinguished, it always allows the words to be heard, an achievement many European composers might learn something from.

Strongly cast, vibrantly played and recorded within weeks of the opera's premiere, Edo De Waart's performance presents the opera in all its multi-layered complexity. De Waart is a long-time champion of Adams' music, and here makes the strongest case for it. The sound is marvellous and the accompanying notes illuminating.

Béla Bartók

Bluebeard's Castle

Samuel Ramey (Bluebeard), Eva Marton (Judith); Hungarian State
Orchestra; Adam Fischer (conductor)

Sony (CBS) CD44523; 1 CD; full price

Bartók wrote just one opera, *Bluebeard's Castle*, a short and intensely concentrated work, and one of very few Hungarian operas to have achieved international fame. Bartók's libretto was written by Béla Balázs, a member of a group of Hungarian intellectuals called the Sunday Circle, who were aware of the developments of the European avant-garde but were also fascinated by their own folk culture – preoccupations that mirrored those of Bartók, who undertook a systematic exploration of Magyar folk song, cultivating a unique musical style in which he treated his native culture as raw material rather than merely a source of atmospheric effects. Balázs's chief sources were Perrault's fairy tale and Maeterlinck's 1901 play *Ariane et Barbe-bleue*, but he also looked at Transylvanian ballads, and the language of his libretto has a regular folk-like metre which is mirrored throughout Bartók's score.

The curtain rises on the entrance hall of Bluebeard's Castle, around which are seven doors. Duke Bluebeard enters with his new wife Judith, who demands to know what lies behind the doors. She opens the first six (revealing his torture chamber, armoury, treasury, garden, kingdom and a lake of tears) before forcing Bluebeard to allow her access to the final doorway. Through this door three women appear: they are the brides of his morning, noon and evening. Judith, the bride of his night, follows her predecessors through the seventh door, leaving Bluebeard alone in the darkness of his castle.

Bartók dedicated *Bluebeard's Castle* to his new bride Márta, a rather ominous dedication in view of the work's affirmation that loneliness is the essential quality of the human condition. The immensely rich and detailed score emphasizes the gulf between Judith and Bluebeard chiefly through the way they sing: dramatic grandeur for her, stark repression for him. Unity is achieved through the statement and repetition of pivotal motifs: for example the theme associated with blood, the interval of a minor second, is employed as the opera's central motif and it accompanies the revealing of every room. For the opening of the various doors Bartók composed highly expressive, miniature tone-poems which encapsulate the contents of each room. The opening of the fifth door is the work's highlight. To convey the white light bursting from Bluebeard's kingdom, there is a simple but staggeringly potent C major chord for orchestra and organ: from this point it is clear that Judith's fate is sealed.

Bluebeard's Castle is at once static and extremely dramatic: its single setting provides a claustrophobic intensity while the gradual unlocking of the doors creates an almost unbearable suspense. Bluebeard and Judith are both seeking a new beginning to their lives, but from the start there is a sense that each of them is on the edge of the void, surrounded by a literal and a metaphorical darkness. It's a mood of anxiety and impending horror similar to that of Schoenberg's contemporary *Erwartung* (see p.145), a work quite often staged as a double bill with *Bluebeard*.

Fischer's sonically spectacular recording of *Bluebeard* features the finest Duke and Judith on record. Eva Marton's soprano is at its best when the throttle is pushed to the floor, but she is able to touch upon lighter textures and darker moods without sounding strained or out of character. Ramey's voice is as large and powerful as Marton's but he too handles the lighter music with care — the fifth door is especially lyrical. Fischer accompanies his singers well, and there's a real glow to the recorded sound. Above all this recording leaves you with an overriding sensation of partnership between the performers.

Ludwig van Beethoven

Fidelio

Christa Ludwig (Leonore), Jon Vickers (Florestan), Walter Berry (Pizarro), Gottlob Frick (Rocco); Philharmonia Chorus and Orchestra; Otto Klemperer (conductor)

EMI CDS5 56211-2; 2 CDs; full price

The composer who wrote his only opera three times, provided it with two titles and four overtures and once grumbled that he found it easier to rework an old composition than begin a new one, was clearly not born to the opera house. *Fidelio* is Beethoven's sole contribution to the genre, perhaps because he found the experience of composing it too draining: it took ten years to bring to a form he thought worthy of his name. Its subject – a wrongfully imprisoned man, Florestan, is saved from execution by his brave and determined wife, Leonore, who disguises herself as a man (Fidelio) to gain work in her husband's prison – dramatizes Beethoven's most profound philosophical beliefs about humanity and redemption, forcing him to the very limits of what music-theatre could express.

Judged purely as a work of theatre *Fidelio* is a long way from being perfect. The structure is lumpen, with spoken dialogue breaking up the arias, ensembles and choruses, and the plot and pacing are predictable. With the exception of Leonore, the characterization is conventional, with a trio of male stereotypes dominated by the most dastardly of villains, the governor Pizarro. And yet, such is the seriousness and intense sincerity of its celebration of love and liberty, *Fidelio* is among the most powerful operas ever written.

The Act I quartet "Mir ist so wunderbar" (So strange I feel) is a perfect example of Beethoven's genius. Not one of the four protagonists – Marzelline, Jacquino, Leonore and Rocco – says anything of any great eloquence, but Beethoven's music, its gentle pulse building to a swell, transmutes the scene: by the end of the quartet you are left aching with sympathy. The monumental "Prisoners' Chorus", in which the briefly liberated men whisper, "We shall be free, we shall find rest" as they emerge into the light, is painfully moving, while Florestan's ten-minute soliloquy at the beginning of Act II, "Gott, welch' Dunkel hier" (God, what darkness is here), is one of the most heart-wrenching of all tenor arias, and has become something of a showpiece. The ecstatic love duet between Florestan and Leonore borders on the religious, and in the final chorus has the transcendent quality of a liturgical setting – indeed, the final ten minutes of *Fidelio*, in which Florestan pays ecstatic homage to his wife's courage, is probably Beethoven's most jubilant music outside his symphonies. To lighten the seriousness of the narrative, Beethoven introduced a dose of characteristically Teutonic wit for the jailer Rocco, and some sweet nothings for the lovers Marzelline and Jacquino, but the weighty central theme is never far away. Wilhelm Furtwängler summed up this opera perfectly when he remarked: "*Fidelio* is, in truth, a Mass rather than an opera. The emotions expressed in the whole of this music touch the borders of religion or are, at least, the constituents of a religion of humanity."

Otto Klemperer's 1962 recording is famous for the old man's powerful conducting and the matchless casting of Vickers and Ludwig as Florestan and Leonore. The former wields his massive tenor with unrivalled intelligence, creating a quasi-religious fervour during the soliloquy and final scene, while Christa Ludwig perfectly captures Leonore's combination of strength and fragility. Gottlob Frick's Rocco is instinctively likable, but the baritone of Walter Berry is rather too expansive to be a truly villainous Pizarro. Klemperer's tempi are on the slow side, but his reading sustains tension even during moments of apparent stasis. On the evidence of this recording the Philharmonia was the 1960s' finest orchestra outside Berlin and Vienna, and EMI's engineers captured them and their celebrated chorus in near perfect sound.

Vincenzo Bellini

La Sonnambula

Joan Sutherland (Amina), Luciano Pavarotti (Elvino), Nicolai Ghiaurov (Rodolfo); London Opera Chorus; National Philharmonic Orchestra; Richard Bonynge (conductor)

Decca 417 424-2DH2; 2 CDs; full price

In the eyes of his contemporaries, Vincenzo Bellini was the very embodiment of the Romantic spirit, a composer who saw himself as an instrument of divine inspiration and his work in terms of its life-changing significance. This heroic self-belief sat at odds with Italian musical culture of the 1830s, when it was common for composers to churn out operas à la Rossini at the rate of one a fortnight. But Bellini expected more of himself and his librettists, and he devoted months to each of the ten operas he completed before his death in 1835, aged just 34. This care and attention is conspicuous throughout *La Sonnambula* (The Sleepwalker), the first of Bellini's operas to achieve world-wide popularity.

Sleepwalking had been used as a plot device by various composers (eg Monteverdi and Mozart) long before Bellini began work on *Sonnambula* in 1831, but he was the first composer to build an entire opera around the phenomenon. The plot is simplicity itself. Amina and Elvino are to marry. Amina's rival, Lisa, tells Elvino that she has seen her flirting with Rodolfo in the tavern. In truth, she was sleepwalking, and her unconscious declarations of love were intended for Elvino. He nonetheless cancels their wedding, and announces his engagement to Lisa. The confusion is resolved, and the lovers reunited, after Amina is seen sleepwalking across the roof of the mill.

Unlike Rossini and Donizetti, who had the facility to make decent operatic music out of a laundry list, Bellini was stumped without a good libretto, and in parts Romani's text for *La Sonnambula* is excellent. It is made outstanding by the music, which represents the apotheosis of the bel canto ("beautiful song") aesthetic, which prized melody above everything else. Indeed, *Sonnambula* is a masterclass in the use of melody for expressive effect, and Glinka was not exaggerating when he noted that early performances of the work drove "audiences to tears of emotion and ecstasy".

Even by his own standards, Bellini's writing for the soprano Amina and the tenor Elvino is outstanding; in pathos and sensitivity they anticipate the intricacy of many of Verdi's finest creations. Amina's Act I cavatina, for example, takes her through jubilation, introversion and anxiety before arriving at an archetypally glittering bel canto display of vocal acrobatics. Similarly expressive is her final number, "Ah, non giunge uman pensiero" (Ah, beyond all human thought), an aria which on its own prompted a revival of interest in *Sonnambula* at the turn of the twentieth century. Elvino is an equally virtuosic role, but his music is extraordinarily languid. His highlight, and one of the most tender scenes in Italian opera, comes in Act I when he hands Amina her engagement ring. The long and delicately spun "Prendi, l'anel ti dono" (Take the ring I give you) may be sentimental, but it is brilliantly effective, and typifies the skill with which Bellini could take a relatively simple eight-bar melody and turn it into something uniquely touching.

On record all that really matters is that the voices are sufficiently captivating to convince the listener that the narrative is not utterly daft, and there are few more beautiful voices than those of Joan Sutherland and Luciano Pavarotti. Neither was in their prime when they recorded the opera in 1980, but this is an almost ideal partnership and together they produce some magical singing. Their attention to questions of style is exactly what Bellini would have wanted, with bags of swooping and sobbing, and thanks to the conductor Richard Bonynge there is sufficient impetus to bind all the pretty tunes together into a dramatic narrative.

Vincenzo Bellini

Norma

Maria Callas (Norma), Mario Filippeschi (Pollione), Ebe Stignani (Adalgisa), Nicola Rossi-Lemeni (Oroveso); La Scala Chorus and Orchestra; Tullio Serafin (conductor)

EMI CDS5 56271-2; 3 CDs; full price

Bellini's incessant appeals to his librettist, Felice Romani, for texts worthy of his theatrical ambitions paid off in 1831 when the writer presented him with *Norma*, perhaps the finest text Bellini ever used, and certainly the one that inspired him to the most thorough integration of words and music. Verbal and musical accents coincide throughout this remarkable opera, which many regard as the finest "singers' opera" in the entire repertoire.

Romani's plot, which tackles the ever-popular themes of forbidden love and divided loyalty, also appealed to the contemporary fascination for Romano-Hellenic subjects. In occupied Gaul, the Roman consul, Pollione, abandons Norma, a Druid princess (by whom he has two sons) for Adalgisa, an acolyte. Neither woman knows of the other's existence, and both are appalled when they make the discovery. Adalgisa, nonetheless, urges Pollione not to abandon the mother of his children. The vengeful Norma, on the other hand, incites the Gauls to war with the Romans. All that is needed is a sacrifice to appease the gods. When Pollione is caught breaking into the Virgins' temple he becomes the unwilling victim. As the sacrificial pyre is lit Norma announces that she will take Pollione's place – an act of such selflessness that Pollione is forced to admit that he has loved her all along. But Norma refuses to stand down, and as she walks into the flames she is joined in death by Pollione.

Unmoved by the self-consciously expert technique of Rossini and bored by much of Donizetti's loquacious melodrama, Bellini was convinced that simple vocal melody was the most effective medium for the portrayal of character, and *Norma* achieves its power through uncomplicated means. Bellini floats enormously long and audaciously exposed lines of song above basic chord progressions. On paper it doesn't amount to much, but the vocal score is extraordinarily beautiful and richly expressive. In particular, the way in which he sustains a continuity between outbursts of vehement emotion and melancholic introversion is utterly compelling. In Act I, for example, Bellini shapes a seamless half-hour dramatic span from the tenor's self-assured showpiece "Mecco all'altar di Venere" (At the altar of Venus), Norma's gloriously poignant prayer for peace, "Casta diva" (Chaste goddess), and Adalgisa's ecstatic resolution to elope with the proconsul, "Va crudele" (Go, cruel woman).

The title role served as the model for many of Verdi's tragic heroines, and when he came to write *Tristan und Isolde* Wagner expressed his wish that Isolde would become his Norma, acknowledging the power of Bellini's creation. And like *Tristan*, *Norma* is an opera of extremes, demanding absolute surrender from an audience – it cannot be appreciated, as can Mozart's operas, by a detached observer. If you listen to this piece sung by a top-quality cast, the last twenty minutes, with their tragic duets for Norma and Pollione, are likely to move you to tears.

If *Norma* is the apotheosis of bel canto tragedy then Maria Callas's 1954 performance for EMI is the apotheosis of recorded interpretations – the skill with which she overcomes the technical difficulties, while immersing herself in the character, has never been surpassed. The occasionally brittle voice will not appeal to everyone, but there is no denying the intensity of this performance. Mario Filippeschi is a wonderfully old-fashioned Pollione, all swoops and sobs, and Ebe Stignani makes an imposing Adalgisa. Serafin keeps a tight grip and the re-mastered CD brings impressive clarity to the early stereo recording.

Vincenzo Bellini

I Puritani

Joan Sutherland (Elvira), Luciano Pavarotti (Arturo), Piero Cappuccilli (Riccardo), Nicolai Ghiaurov (Giorgio); Chorus of the Royal Opera House; London Symphony Orchestra; Richard Bonynge (conductor)

Decca 417 588-2DH2; 3 CDs; full price

"Carve in your head in letters of adamant: the music drama must draw tears, inspire terror, make people die." So the exasperated Bellini wrote to Count Carlo Pepoli, his librettist for *I Puritani*. Their partnership was brought about by Rossini, who had made songs from some of the Count's poetry. Rossini's attitude to the relationship between language and music was rather more devil-may-care than Bellini's and, initially at least, Bellini regretted the collaboration. But the weakness of the text forced the composer to work that much harder, and he ennobled Pepoli's efforts with some of the finest, most expressive music of his career, turning a sow's ear into one of opera's most silky purses.

For their subject Bellini and Pepoli turned, like many Italian composers of the time, to Walter Scott – in this case his Civil War novel of 1816, *Old Mortality*. The British context can have meant little to Italian audiences, but the drama's themes of nationalism, rebellion and liberty struck a chord with a populace under foreign rule. The drama unfolds in Plymouth: Arturo, a Cavalier, loves Elvira, a Puritan (Roundhead). When he rescues the captive Queen by dressing her in Elvira's bridal veil, Elvira believes herself betrayed and goes mad. Arturo is arrested by his rival in love, Riccardo, and is sentenced to death – which shocks Elvira back to her senses. Arturo and Elvira embrace for what seems the last time, when news arrives of the Stuarts' defeat. The war is over, and the pardoned Arturo and Elvira are free to marry.

I Puritani is something of a bel canto manifesto, with an emotional range that goes a long way towards compensating for Pepoli's shortcomings. From Arturo's languid and haunting "A te o cara" (To you, my dear) to sparkling coloratura arias such as Elvira's lustrous "Son vergin vezzosa" (I am a gentle virgin), this opera flaunts an array of set-pieces that's without equal in the bel canto repertoire, and the only reason *I Puritani* doesn't come around very often is that there are very, very few singers able to sing the lead roles. "A te o cara", with which Arturo makes his first entrance, calls for a high C sharp; his exuberant duet with Elvira, "Vieni, fra questa braccia" (Come into my arms), has two high Ds; and, as if that weren't enough, the final, tear-jerking duet with Elvira, "Credeasi, misera" (She believed, unhappy girl), calls for a high F – way above the top note of *Turandot's* "Nessun dorma". To stabilize the vocal coruscations, Bellini provided an unusually sophisticated orchestral accompaniment, with expressive changes in key and metre, and harmonies that are much more adventurous than in his previous works. *I Puritani* may lack the dramatic cohesion of *Norma*, but judged as an assemblage of vocal highlights it is one of the most enjoyable operas of its period.

Pavarotti made his official debut in 1961, and for the first fifteen years of his career he made his reputation specializing in little-heard bel canto repertoire. In 1974, when he made this remarkable recording of *I Puritani*, he was at the height of his powers and there are few more extraordinary examples of the lyric tenor's art. The voice is sumptuous and the ease with which he launches himself into the many high notes is staggering. Joan Sutherland had already recorded Elvira for Decca, but her second reading is vastly superior, with finer diction, a greater expressive range and an ensemble sensitivity that brings much-needed concentration to the opera. Piero Cappuccilli is a fine Riccardo and Richard Bonynge ensures that the whole thing keeps moving.

Alban Berg

Wozzeck

Franz Grundheber (Wozzeck), Waltraud Meier (Marie), Graham Clark (The Captain), Günter von Kannen (The Doctor), Endrik Wottrich (Andres); Chorus and Orchestra of the Berlin State Opera; Daniel Barenboim (conductor)

Teldec 0630-14108-2; 2 CDs; full price

Georg Büchner's play *Woyzeck* – which was more than seventy years old when Berg first saw it – is a powerful indictment of military brutality and a painful unravelling of the social pressures that might lead an ordinary man to murder. This ordinary man, Woyzeck (Wozzeck in Berg's version), is first seen shaving the Captain, who ridicules and humiliates him for fathering a child out of wedlock. Wozzeck replies that virtue is something that only the rich can afford. He then suffers at the hands of his mercenary and faithless mistress Marie, a Doctor who is using him as a guinea-pig for his experiments, and a Drum-Major, who beats him for refusing to drink with him. Driven to distraction by Marie's infatuation with the Drum-Major and the Drum-Major's boasting, Wozzeck stabs Marie to death. He throws the blade into a lake; haunted by visions and fearful that someone may find the weapon, he returns to the lake, where he drowns.

Berg used Büchner's text more or less word for word, telescoping the action into fifteen fast-moving cinematic scenes. Each of the characters is sharply drawn, and each of the adults is implicated in Wozzeck's tragedy. Only Marie's child is innocent, but with Marie dead, the other children predict that her offspring too is doomed to a life of pain and submission. It was this fatalistic conclusion, as much as the abrasively modern music, that angered the Nazis, who banned the opera in 1933.

Wozzeck is Berg's most expressionistic work, with a largely dissonant score that creates an atmosphere of mounting paranoia and oppressiveness. But the music is more varied than such a summary suggests, for there are outbreaks of more reassuring and lyrical music (in Marie's lullaby for instance) as well as a Mahlerian tendency to parody simple musical genres for ironic effect, above all in the nightmarish tavern scene. Throughout the work Berg makes brilliantly subtle use of *Sprechgesang* (speech-song), a style in which the rhythm and pitch of every note is carefully prescribed – although Berg favours a more fluid vocal manner than Schoenberg, leaving the choice of tonal colour up to the performer.

The three acts are performed without intervals, with terse orchestral interludes played during scene changes. Berg makes use of academic musical forms, such as a sonata or a fugue, to unify the individual scenes, and employs leitmotifs to tie the whole work together, the most prominent of these being the one associated with Wozzeck's predicament as a poor man who cannot afford morality – a motif that acquires new potency in the final interlude, a luscious post-Romantic summation of the entire tragedy. However, Berg insisted that "No matter how thorough one's knowledge of the musical forms which are to be found within the opera . . . from the moment when the curtain rises until it falls for the last time, nobody in the audience ought to notice anything of these forms – everyone should be filled only by the idea of the opera, an idea which far transcends the individual fate of Wozzeck."

Barenboim's live 1994 recording of *Wozzeck* is outstanding even by his standards. No other conductor has such an instinctive feel for Berg's fastidious orchestrations while at the same time highlighting the enormous architectural structures that sustain the three acts. Franz Grundheber is ideal in the title role, as alive to the character's self-pity as to his rage, and Waltraud Meier is electrifying as Marie. Graham Clark and Günter von Kannen are memorably horrible as the Captain and the Doctor, and the orchestra respond to Barenboim with the clarity of a chamber ensemble.

Alban Berg

Lulu

Teresa Stratas (Lulu), Franz Mazura (Dr Schön), Kurt Riegel (Alwa), Yvonne Minton (Countess Geschwitz); Paris Opera Orchestra; Pierre Boulez (conductor)

Deutsche Grammophon 415 489–2GH3; 3 CDs; full price

While Strauss's *Salome* (see p.153) epitomizes the fantasy of the destructive allure of female sexuality, Berg's *Lulu* is a rather more complex and less paranoiac representation of that *fin de siècle* archetype, the femme fatale. Frank Wedekind's "Lulu" plays (*Earthspirit* and *Pandora's Box*) were regarded as so shocking that they were banned in Germany between 1905 and 1918. Berg first saw them in a private performance in 1905, and immediately recognized a world-view that was congruent with his own, and which he later sketched in a letter to his fiancée Helene Nahowski: "sensuality is not a weakness, does not mean a surrender to one's own will. Rather it is an immense strength – the pivot of all our being and thinking."

If the world is a menagerie, as the Animal Tamer suggests in the opening monologue, then sexuality is what motivates it. But the character of Lulu, unlike Don Giovanni, is an amoral representation of the pleasure principle – she is the embodiment of pure desire rather than of moral transgression. Moreover, though she is in many ways inscrutable in her motives, Lulu is a self-determining woman, and it is her very independence, her refusal to abide by the rules of men, that leads to her death.

Berg decided to stick closely to Wedekind's texts, a decision that produced an elliptical and self-consciously episodic plot which is almost overloaded with demi-monde archetypes: bloated plutocrat, aspiring artist, down-and-out, etc. In Act I Lulu's elderly husband, Dr Goll, dies of a stroke, and she is raped by her portrait painter. Lulu then marries the Painter, but secretly carries on an affair with Dr Schön. When the Painter kills himself after hearing of her infidelity, Lulu and Schön marry. In Act II various admirers try to seduce Lulu, including the Countess Geschwitz, Schön's son Alwa and a schoolboy. When Schön finds Lulu and Alwa together he demands that Lulu shoot herself. Instead, she turns the pistol on Schön. Lulu is arrested, convicted and sent to jail, but she and Alwa fall in love and escape together to Paris and later London, where she lives as a prostitute. One of her clients turns out to be Jack the Ripper, who cuts Lulu's throat.

As in *Wozzeck*, Berg binds together the work's disparate elements through a wealth of structural devices – leitmotifs, sonata form, rondo, variations. The score of *Lulu* is something of a masterclass in compositional technique, but this is not to say the opera is opaque to those who cannot perceive the intricate constructions beneath the welter of sound – the interconnections operate principally on a subliminal level. Heard in the theatre or on record, Lulu makes its impact through its almost overwhelming sonic richness, as it ranges from Straussian full-orchestral density to parodic pared-down Berlin cabaret – indeed, Stravinsky identified "the saxophone's juvenile-deliquent personality" as the identifying characteristic of "the vast decadence of *Lulu*."

The opera's orchestration was unfinished when Berg died, and it was only in 1979, when Pierre Boulez premiered a version of *Lulu* completed by Friedrich Cerha, that the three-act *Lulu* was at last heard. The finest recording was produced in the wake of that premiere, with much the same team as performed the work at the Paris Opéra. Teresa Stratas made something of a reputation for herself playing neurotic heroines, and her portrayal of Lulu is justifiably celebrated for its intensity. Her supporting cast are no less committed, with a particularly chilling performance from Franz Mazura as Dr Schön. The Paris Orchestra play like demons and Boulez directs the massive enterprise with a vice-like grip.

Hector Berlioz

La Damnation de Faust

Keith Lewis (Faust), Bryn Terfel (Méphistophélès), Anne Sofie von Otter (Marguérite); Philharmonia Chorus and Orchestra; Myng-Whun Chung (conductor)

Deutsche Grammophon 453 500-2; 2 CDs; full price

"My life is a deeply interesting romance." So wrote Hector Berlioz (1803–69), a composer so conscious of his own significance that he poured himself not only into his music but also into a Byronic autobiography that is as entertaining as it is unreliable. This romantic self-absorption was fuelled by a number of early influences, chiefly Shakespeare and Virgil, but he spent most of his life standing – so he believed – in the shadow of Beethoven, whose death in 1827 came as a terrible shock to him. But Berlioz's operatic style owed little to the Teutonic gravity of *Fidelio* (see p.5); rather, it sprang from the lavish theatricality of Grand Opéra composers such as Meyerbeer, Spontini and Cherubini, men who had their eyes trained firmly on the box office. But in spite of his fondness for large-scale drama Berlioz was not someone to confine himself within the boundaries of popular taste, and even his grandest opera – *Les Troyens* – is distinguished by a subtlety and depth of character not normally associated with the five-act mythological operas of the type produced by Meyerbeer and his ilk.

He was inspired to write the first of his four operas in 1831 by the swashbuckling autobiography of the Renaissance sculptor Benvenuto Cellini, one of the few books that can stand comparison with Berlioz's engagingly self-aggrandizing memoirs.

Unfortunately, this two-act masterpiece was a flop at its premiere, a setback which – not for the last time – Berlioz blamed on the production rather than his work. In response he conceived his next theatrical project, an operatic interpretation of the Faust myth, for the concert stage, creating a unique genre he termed "opéra de concert". Taking as its source Part One of Goethe's *Faust*, *La Damnation de Faust* (1846) tells the tale of the necromancer who summons the Devil to end his misery and loneliness, which he does through the winsome figure of Marguérite. Berlioz set out to create a piece in which – true to the character of Goethe's poem – the coherence derives from the themes of the work rather than from a linear narrative, and he wanted his music to conjure all the images traditionally left to stagecraft. *La Damnation de Faust* is an astoundingly inventive sound-world, evoking everything from "the whole of Nature" (Berlioz's typically lofty phrase to describe his depiction of the elements) to a ride on winged horses into the mouth of Hell. The work is not all about pictorialism, however, for Berlioz demonstrates throughout his remarkable gift for text-setting. The song-like intimacy of much of the writing for Faust's tenor and Marguérite's soprano is of a delicacy you don't find in the blood-and-thunder of most French romantic opera, though Berlioz did indulge his more bombastic instincts when writing for the gaudy figure of Méphistophélès.

The most recent recording of *Faust* is in many respects the best. The stellar cast is led by veteran tenor Keith Lewis, whose interpretation of the title role, while less obviously beautiful than many of his rivals, is considerably more dramatic, and he brings genuine anguish and horror to the necromancer's fall. As his adversary, Bryn Terfel hams it up nicely, with just enough malice to offset the generosity that is the hallmark of this wonderful voice. Anne Sofie von Otter is probably the most effortless Marguérite on record, and she tackles the role's awkward range with remarkable confidence. Chung's attention to the music's extremes (particularly the hair-raising ride into Hell) generates a tremendous sense of theatre. The sound is vital and the orchestra play superbly.

Hector Berlioz

Les Troyens

Jon Vickers (Aeneas), Josephine Veasey (Dido); Royal Opera House Chorus and Orchestra; Colin Davis (conductor)

Philips 416 432-2PH4; 4 CDs; full price

Encouraged by the success of *Faust*, Berlioz embarked on a project that was even more ambitious – an opera about the Trojan Wars. Taking his text from the *Aeneid*, he spent two years labouring on the massive score, and the effort nearly killed him. According to his calculations, a complete performance of *Les Troyens* (including an interval) would last just short of six hours, but he did not live to see anything more than the last three of the five acts, the first performance of which – in 1863 – resulted in a hostile response from the press. The first two acts were not performed until 1890, and the first complete *Troyens* had to wait until a century after his death, when Colin Davis conducted a centenary production at Covent Garden.

The motivation for turning Virgil into an operatic epic came from one of Franz Liszt's lovers, the Princess Sayn-Wittgenstein, who in 1855 told Berlioz of Wagner's ambition to write a four-part cycle of operas. But where Wagner was working towards the creation of a radically modern and fluid form of music-drama, Berlioz wanted to return to the play-like structures and classical architecture of the era of Gluck (see p.61), which he believed better suited to the austerity and grandeur of Virgil's verses.

Les Troyens' musical style is indebted to Gluck in that there are almost no opportunities for virtuoso vocal display. The score does make punishing demands – particularly of the lovers Dido and Aeneas – but they are entirely at the service of the drama. This epic-scale opera is extremely difficult to produce, not least because of the frequent and drastic scene changes, and Berlioz himself virtually invited criticism of the opera's construction, for throughout his piano version of the score he makes numerous suggestions as to what might be cut for performance. However, the intensely lyrical and dazzlingly orchestrated music goes some way to draw attention away from the episodic structure, and a single theme (taken from the "Trojan March" at the end of Act III) occurs at key moments to lend cohesion when needed most. Characterization is subjugated to the concept of humanity as a component of the vast machinery of history, yet the vocal writing is consistently beautiful, especially for Dido (mezzo) and Aeneas (tenor) – indeed "Dido's Lament" is perhaps the most affecting mezzo-soprano aria in all French opera. The eminent critic Winton Dean once wrote: "the series of adjacent blocks from which the operas are constructed frequently seem as if they have been conceived without reference to each other. When placed in succession they resemble . . . a window of exquisite stained glass incompletely leaded." There's some justice to this criticism, but judged on the merits of its parts, *Les Troyens* is among the most thrilling operas of the nineteenth century, for Berlioz's orchestration is the work of a magician, his melodies are captivating, and his flair for text-setting improves even the limpest bits of dialogue.

Colin Davis's 1969 recording for Philips is still the benchmark. Made with his Covent Garden forces, this performance has a conviction and security that defies criticism. Davis is generally a cautious conductor, and this reticence was to serve him well with Berlioz's huge work, for he concentrates on binding together the unwieldy structure, rather than on underlining the highlights. His cast is lead by Jon Vickers, one of the world's greatest tenors, and by the under-appreciated Josephine Veasey, who captures both the fragility and the strength of Virgil's heroine. The huge supporting cast is excellent (particularly Ian Partridge's Iopas) and the orchestra and chorus are as one.

Leonard Bernstein

Candide

Jerry Hadley (Candide), June Anderson (Cunegonde), Christa Ludwig (Old Lady), Adolph Green (Dr Pangloss); London Symphony Chorus and Orchestra; Leonard Bernstein (conductor)

Deutsche Grammophon 429 734-2GH2; 2 CDs; full price.

Leonard Bernstein followed the lead of George Gershwin (see p.55) in trying to break down the division between the world of the American musical and the world of opera. His most successful attempt was the comic-operetta *Candide*, composed after Voltaire, between 1954 and 1956, to a libretto by Lillian Hellman, Richard Wilbur, Dorothy Parker, John Latouche and at least four uncredited writers. Despite rave reviews, its premiere on Broadway was a flop, and Bernstein embarked on revisions and re-revisions. In 1973 it re-emerged, with a libretto overhauled by Hugh Wheeler and Stephen Sondheim. This new version was a hit and it remained the performing edition until 1988 when, in collaboration with Bernstein, the conductor John Mauceri produced an "opera house" version, which the composer recorded the year before his death in 1990.

Voltaire's *Candide*, first published in 1759, is a riposte to Leibniz's optimistic philosophy that "all is for the best in the best of all possible worlds". It was Lillian Hellman's idea to turn it into a work of music-theatre – she regarded it as "the greatest satire ever written, hitting out in all directions, enclosing all human nonsense", undoubtedly thinking of her own experiences at the hands of the virulent Congressional committee headed by Senator McCarthy. Bernstein largely shared her left-of-centre liberal humanism, and on one level Candide functions as a critique of 1950s America, though a scene ridiculing McCarthy was removed and its ultimately positive ending differs from Voltaire's consistently sceptical vision. The narrative follows the travels of Candide and Cunegonde, who have been taught by Dr Pangloss that the world is a wonderful place. However, their experiences of exile, war, rape, the Inquisition and betrayal lead them to a new, less naive understanding of the world, and they return home to a life without Pangloss, in which they strive to "make their gardens grow".

Fans of musicals might, with some justification, rate the dramatic qualities of Bernstein's *West Side Story* above those of *Candide*, but the latter is the superior work in many respects and it is a shame that its stylistic diversity has prevented it from taking root in the international repertory. *Candide* can be taken as Bernstein's frenetic homage to the richness of the European and American musical traditions. From the glittering overture (with its marvellous send-up of Brahms) through solemn chorales to parodies of Offenbach and Gounod, jazz riffs, tangos, waltzes and love songs cut from the original draft of *West Side Story*'s "Maria" and "Tonight", *Candide* is a glorious rag-bag. At times the cake does seem over-egged, and there is a fair dose of unintentionally comic sincerity, but the mixture of popular and classical is deftly balanced and, on the whole, tremendous fun. Highlights include the coloratura aria "Glitter and be Gay", the absurd "Oh, Happy We" and the concluding "Make our Garden Grow", in which Bernstein gave full rein to his predilection for the sentimental.

It is a measure of Bernstein's celebrity that he was able to secure three of the biggest names in opera for this 1989 recording. Christa Ludwig (as the Old Lady) and Nicolai Gedda (in various roles) were both approaching retirement, but their star quality is in evidence throughout. June Anderson (a regular at La Scala and the Met) is ideal as Cunegonde, and the tenor Jerry Hadley is youthful and fresh-voiced in the title role. Most of the rest of the cast is outstanding, and Bernstein manages to generate a decidedly un-English fizz from the LSO and chorus.

Harrison Birtwistle

Punch and Judy

Stephen Roberts (Punch), Jan DeGaetani (Judy/Fortune-Teller), Philip Langridge (Lawyer), Phyllis Bryn-Julson (Pretty Polly/Witch), David Wilson-Johnson (Choregos/Jack Ketch), John Tomlinson (Doctor); London Sinfonietta; David Atherton (conductor)

Etcetera KTC 2014; 2 CDs; full price

Harrison Birtwistle's first stage work was commissioned by and first performed during the 1968 Aldeburgh Festival, where it achieved instant notoriety by provoking the festival's guiding spirit, Benjamin Britten, to walk out in disgust. Many were appalled by all the wailing, clanging and violence, with one critic attacking *Punch and Judy* as "gratuitously offensive". For others, however, it was an uncompromising and welcome assault on the comfortable certainties of the English tradition – revealing, in its grotesque re-invention of end-of-the-pier children's entertainment, the barbarities lurking just under the surface of certain aspects of traditional English culture.

Typical of this and Birtwistle's immediately subsequent works for the stage is the lack of linear narrative: the story is not told in sequence from beginning to end, but nightmarishly re-enacted over and over again, each time from a slightly different angle, creating a tension between the heated, bloody subject matter and its dispassionate, rather alienated presentation. Punch is rocking the baby, then throws it into the fire. He stabs Judy to death when she finds the charred baby. Punch is now free to seek Pretty Polly, and he leaves on his horse. He finds her and offers her a flower, which she refuses, saying it was tarnished by his murder of the baby. The Doctor and Lawyer revile Punch, but they too are murdered and join Judy at the chorus gibbet. Punch again woos Pretty Polly, giving her a prism. Again she rejects him. Punch murders the Choregos, a narrator figure. This is a turning point in Punch's life. He is haunted by nightmarish images of his cruelty and a satanic wedding with Judy. Punch goes to the gallows for his crimes, but cheats the hangman. Pretty Polly reappears and the two sing a love duet around the gallows, now transformed into a maypole.

Though Birtwistle's use of truncated toccatas, arias, recitatives, quartets and chorales applies the Baroque doctrine of "one mood per movement" to Punch's brutal progress, the sound-world of this *commedia dell'arte* horror-story is stridently new. The vocal writing requires the performers to sing way out of their natural ranges, and Birtwistle's characteristically aggressive score is especially notable for its percussive qualities, which can be thrilling in much the same way that a hail-storm can be thrilling. Providing some sort of anchor, various musical signposts punctuate the action: each murder is prefaced by the line "The sweetness of the moment is undeniably bitter"; recurrent "Passion Chorales", in which Judy, the Doctor and Lawyer comment on what's just happened, are a distancing device that heightens the horror of Punch's rampage while invoking the precedent of ancient Greek drama; and duets, lullabies and dances act as lyrical counterpoints to the mayhem. *Punch and Judy* is modern opera's most frighteningly vivid portrayal of the Freudian id in all its cruelty and lustfulness.

David Atherton, who conducted the first performance, gives a brisk and pungent account of this opera, with an orchestra for whom this music is second nature. The clarity of the textures and the vibrancy of the attack are remarkable, and Atherton's evident enthusiasm for the score brings an immediacy to the performance essential if it is to have the necessary impact. Veteran baritone Stephen Roberts is full-bloodedly horrible as Punch, Jan DeGaetani is a suitably tormented Judy and a galaxy of British operatic talent takes on the secondary parts. The recording is clear, if a little bit flat, but this is the only reservation to be made about this intrepid venture.

Harrison Birtwistle

Gawain

François Le Roux (Gawain), Anne Howells (Lady de Hautdesert), Marie Angel (Morgan Le Fay), John Tomlinson (The Green Knight), Penelope Walmsley-Clarke (Guinevere); Chorus and Orchestra of the Royal Opera House; Elgar Howarth (conductor)

Collins Classics 70412; 2 CDs; full price

Harrison Birtwistle polarizes audiences more than any other post-war British composer. The extreme responses provoked by his work have brought him world-wide notoriety, and his music – though unknown in the vast majority of households – is regularly performed throughout Europe and North America. It was a measure of his significance that in 1990 the Royal Opera House, Covent Garden, felt able to commission his *Gawain* – a colossal, three-hour opera based on the anonymous fourteenth-century epic poem *Sir Gawain and the Green Knight*. The first production in 1991 created a sensation – as much for the score as its staging, which brought the latest technology to the beheadings and talking heads – and it is now one of the most frequently performed new operas of the last twenty years.

Birtwistle and his librettist David Harsent present the ancient drama as a through-composed narrative – which was something of a departure for the composer. The tale is simple: the Green Knight arrives at the court of King Arthur and challenges any one of the knights to decapitate him with a single blow of an axe; Gawain steps forward and cleaves the Knight's head from his body. The knight picks up his head and rides away, having promised that they will meet again in exactly one year's time so that he can return the blow. Gawain seeks out the Knight, encounters the lovely Lady de Hautdesert, and survives the duel, if only to learn that he is an ordinary man, not the hero he once thought himself to be.

Birtwistle's fascination with the story of Gawain and the Green Knight is rooted in the poem's presentation of the changing seasons and its almost pantheistic world-view – a preoccupation with such matters was first revealed in his dramatic pastoral *Down by the Greenwood Side*, which handled themes of death and rebirth with urgent, black humour, and has remained an almost constant feature of his output. With the slow revolution of the year and Gawain's arduous journey constituting the foundations of *Gawain*, Birtwistle's music has a greater sense of organic development than did *Punch and Judy*, and in its lush harmonies and complex, high-volume orchestration you might – if you listen carefully – hear something of the sound-worlds of late Romanticism. However, Birtwistle's counterpoint is so complex that, at times, a dozen separate strands are at work simultaneously, and the end result is something like a sonic battering ram, as Birtwistle applies layer after layer of music in building one thunderous climax after another. There's the odd episode of tenderness, like the scene between Gawain and Lady de Hautdesert, but there is generally very little contrast throughout the opera's length. The vocal score is more often than not written as an orchestral voice, winding its way within, rather than above, the instrumentation, but at full tilt (as in the Knight's hypnotic Act I monologue) *Gawain* is absorbing music-theatre.

Collins's live recording of *Gawain* was taken from a performance of Birtwistle's 1994 revision at Covent Garden, in which the huge orchestral interlude called "The Turning of the Seasons" was truncated. The baritone François Le Roux created the title role, and he soars through it with noble ease. Marie Angel copes magnificently with the extremely difficult soprano role of Morgan Le Fay and bass John Tomlinson produces a scene-stealing performance as the Green Knight. Elgar Howarth does his best to allow some light into the omnipresent shade, and the Covent Garden chorus and orchestra deserve medals for their virtuoso performance of Birtwistle's unrelenting score.

Georges Bizet

Carmen

Teresa Berganza (Carmen), Placido Domingo (Don José), Ileana Cotrubas (Micaëla), Sherrill Milnes (Escamillo); Ambrosian Singers; London Symphony Orchestra; Claudio Abbado (conductor)

Deutsche Grammophon DG 419 636; 3 CDs; full price

Bizet once wrote in a letter, "I tell you that if you were to suppress adultery, fanaticism, crime, evil and the supernatural, there would no longer be the means for writing one note." This credo was given substance with *Carmen*, an opera that came as a shock to the first-night audience at the Opéra-Comique, a theatre in which the traditional diet was somewhat lighter than this tale of erotic obsession and murder. *Carmen* is the great forerunner of *verismo* opera, the hot-blooded genre typified by *Cavallaria rusticana* (see p.89) and *I Pagliacci* (see p.83), but there's far more to *Carmen* than the venting of passions – its earthy vitality is the product of a hugely sophisticated musician. And, as Bizet was quick to point out, the success of his last opera owed as much to the pungency of its plot (taken from Prosper Mérimée's novella) as to his music: Carmen seduces the soldier Don José (who is loved by the solid but unexciting Micaëla), only to drop him for the bull-fighter Escamillo; driven mad by jealousy, Don José stabs Carmen to death.

"If you want to learn how to orchestrate, don't study Wagner's scores, study the score of *Carmen*." So wrote Richard Strauss, and indeed Bizet's orchestration is outstandingly inventive. Whereas wind instruments had conventionally just provided a bit of colour, here they are used to state leading themes, as in the *seguidilla* and the "Flower Song", while violins are used to imitate guitars and mimic a sliding vocal manner. Individual instruments are also used to emphasize character and Bizet's sophisticated use of motifs helps tie the score together. Local colour is achieved with spicy dissonances, sliding harmonies, and some of the liveliest rhythms in all opera. The dances and gypsy songs create a thrilling synthesis of Spanish culture, even though most of the "authentic" tunes are the composer's own invention.

Carmen herself is one of the great mezzo roles, and her manipulative and magnetic personality is articulated through music of graphic sensuality – her opening *habañera* and *seguidilla* are especially sexy. Her hyperbolic sensuality emphasizes the plodding egotism of the muscle-bound baritone Escamillo, whose music is typified by the swaggering "Toreador Song", while his conceited and two-dimensional character highlights the complexities of the impulsive tenor Don José, the emotional axis of the drama. Don José's disintegration – revealed through music that moves from the tender Act I duet with Micaëla, via the impassioned plea to Carmen (the "Flower Song") to the ravings of his final confrontation with his "demon" – is a masterpiece of progressive characterization. The tempestuous relationship between Don José and Carmen culminates in one of opera's most gripping finales. Resisting the temptation to end his work with an unbroken song (as was then the fashion), Bizet constructs a duet of short and powerful exchanges, a fitful dialogue that conveys the fracturing of José's mind as powerfully as it does the shallowness of Carmen's affections. The culmination, in which he howls one final cry of devotion to the corpse at his feet, is amazingly intense.

The Abbado recording is a superbly professional *Carmen*, featuring some of the best singers the world had to offer in 1977. Domingo is a smooth but powerful Don José, Teresa Berganza is a very sexy Carmen, vocally magnificent and suggesting a youthful capriciousness so often missing from modern interpretations. Sherrill Milnes struts through the role of Escamillo and delivers his "Toreador Song" with splendid oomph, while Ileana Cotrubas is a vibrant if unusually weighty Micaëla. The orchestra and chorus come from London, but they play a vital part in making this the most Spanish *Carmen* on record.

Alexander Borodin

Prince Igor

Mikhail Kit (Prince Igor), Galina Gorchakova (Yaroslavna), Gegam Grigorian (Vladimir), Olga Borodina (Konchakovna); Kirov Theatre Chorus and Orchestra; Valery Gergiev (conductor)

Philips 442 537-2PH3; 3 CDs; full price

Borodin once wrote that in opera "bold outlines only are necessary". *Prince Igor*, his one completed opera, is indeed a work in which bold outlines dominate, and its grand gestures and melodramatic passions – the antithesis of Mussorgsky's bleak, slow-moving *Boris Godounov* (see p.111) – ally it more closely to the work of Borodin's Italian contemporaries, chiefly Verdi, than to his Russian contemporaries. At heart Borodin was a lyrical composer, unmoved by what he called the "mystical ramblings" of Mussorgsky, and although *Igor's* plot – created by Vladimir Stasov, the pre-eminent Russian critic of the time – carried a powerful nationalist message, Borodin was more interested in the drama's individual relationships than in the issues of nationality, creed and politics with which Stasov littered his text. As Rimsky-Korsakov remarked, Borodin was at best a "reluctant patriot".

The drama unfolds in twelfth-century Russia. Igor and his son Vladimir leave Yaroslavna, Igor's wife, to fight the Tartar Polovtsi tribe. They are defeated and taken prisoner by the Polovtsian Khan, Konchak. Vladimir falls in love with Konchak's daughter, Konchakovna, who urges her father to secure peace with Igor. Igor wishes to continue the war, however, and escapes. The opera ends in jubilation at Igor's safe return, tinged with uncertainty, as Konchak resolves to march on Russia.

Borodin's love of Italian opera is manifest throughout the essentially upbeat score, chiefly in the smooth bel canto lines of Vladimir and Konchakovna's love music, and in the comic passages involving the secondary roles of Skula and Eroshka (drunken deserters from Igor's army). The lively overture and wonderfully manic "Polovtsian Dances", with their piquant harmonies, brittle rhythms and exotic intervals, are rather more Russian-sounding, but there's nothing here to compare with the ethnic authenticity for which Mussorgsky strove.

Igor's weakness is not its music, which tears along with great melodic vigour, but its construction, which was undoubtedly marred by the eighteen-year gestation (1869–1887), during which Borodin patched together his libretto while repeatedly reworking the music. Characters come and go with little purpose, and the apparently central figure of Igor's brother, Prince Galitsky, disappears completely after the first act. Furthermore, while each scene is impressive in isolation, they fail to cohere as a work of narrative theatre. It didn't help that Borodin died leaving many parts unfinished. It was left to the ever-industrious Rimsky-Korsakov – together with Glazunov, who scored the overture from his memory of a single performance by Borodin at the piano – to make the score presentable for the first performance, in 1890, three years after the composer's death. For all its lumpiness, however, *Prince Igor* is a genuinely epic work, and much easier to digest than many epics, thanks to a verve and warmth that's rare in Russian opera of this period.

Valery Gergiev's *Prince Igor*, recorded after a 1993 production, is one of the highlights of his Kirov Opera series for Philips. All the constituent parts are as they should be, and Gergiev propels the drama with outrageous gusto, pushing his players and chorus to the limits. Mikhail Kit's ringing bass may lack definition, but as a vocal character-actor he creates an ideal portrayal of the title role. Galina Gorchakova's wonderful dramatic soprano brings sweetness and dignity to Yaroslavna. Even if Gegam Grigorian tries too hard as Vladimir, the love music proves that he can curb his heroic tenor when he tries. The high production standards round off one of the great opera recordings of the 1990s.

Benjamin Britten

Peter Grimes

Jon Vickers (Grimes), Heather Harper (Ellen Orford), Norman Bailey
(Captain Balstrode); Royal Opera House Chorus and Orchestra; Colin
Davis (conductor)

Philips 432 578-2PM2; 2 CDs; mid-price

Benjamin Britten was the most
significant British-born composer
since Henry Purcell (see p.129)
and the nation's most prolific opera
composer. At least five of his thirteen operas have secured a place in
the mainstream repertory and all of
them have been recorded at least
twice. In particular, *Peter Grimes* is
widely regarded as the most
important modern British contri-
bution to the genre. Its premiere in 1945 marked a turning point
in British musical culture, proving the existence of an audience for
good contemporary work, and providing an inspiration for young
British composers such as Michael Tippett (see p.167).

Grimes is based on George Crabbe's "The Borough", a poem
which, with the character of the outcast Peter Grimes, offered
Britten a protagonist with whom he immediately identified. At
the outset of the opera the fisherman Grimes is already alienated
from the Borough because an apprentice has died in his care.
Ellen Orford, a schoolmistress, pleads with him to leave with
her. He refuses, and takes on another apprentice – who, it
appears, is then treated brutally by Grimes. When this boy disappears, the local people conclude that Grimes is a murderer. He is
told by one of the villagers to take his boat out to sea and sink it.
The following morning the coast guard reports a sunken vessel,
and life in the Borough returns to normal.

Peter Grimes remains the composer's most popular stage work, but it's an extremely harsh and emotionally ambiguous opera, which asks us to sympathize with a violent and irascible man, simply because of the merciless way he is judged and isolated by the community. Grimes is the ostensible protagonist, but the Borough itself is the most powerful human entity, exercising a largely negative power that even defeats Ellen Orford, whose love offers Grimes his one hope of redemption. Overwhelming everyone, however, is the sea itself – the famous "Sea Interludes", used at the beginning and middle of each act, establish the constant presence of the sea as the opera's dominant force, and are among the most brilliantly evocative music that Britten ever wrote.

Despite the conventional framework of orchestral interludes, a storm scene and a mad scene, *Peter Grimes* is a peculiarly twentieth-century opera in the way it depicts the central tragedy in terms of an intolerant society that victimizes non-conformity. Even so, Grimes is a morally disturbing character in a way that the central character of Berg's *Wozzeck* (an influence on Britten's opera) is not, and although he's not the psychopath of Crabbe's poem his precise involvement in the death of his first apprentice is left unclear. Certainly Britten gives him the finest music, with the enraptured vision of the soliloquy "Now the Great Bear and Pleiades" in Act I giving a crucial insight into his troubled psyche. But this poetic singularity is in stark contrast to the cruelty with which he treats his new apprentice in Act II, which in turn gives way to the poignant reverie "In dreams I've built myself some kindlier home".

The composer's own recording is superb, but Peter Pears's tenor is too light to carry the title role's descent into despair and madness. Much finer is Jon Vickers' colossal performance for Colin Davis. His is a terrifying portrayal of Grimes's frustration, displaying a mixture of violence, anguish and fragility that has a Lear-like quality. Heather Harper makes an earthy Ellen Orford, and the supporting cast are uniformly excellent. Davis lacks Britten's confident drive, and you might wish for greater momentum, but he brings out the colours of the score beautifully.

Benjamin Britten

Albert Herring

Peter Pears (Albert), Sylvia Fisher (Lady Billows), Catherine Wilson (Nancy), Joseph Ward (Sid); English Chamber Orchestra; Benjamin Britten (conductor)

Decca 421 849-2LH2; 2 CDs; full price

Benjamin Britten began *Albert Herring* in 1946, a year after the first performance of *Peter Grimes*, a work that can be regarded as its tragic converse. Both operas play on small-town dynamics and attitudes, and deal with the issue of social isolation within an inward-looking community, a predicament with which Britten – a homosexual and conscientious objector – was intensely sympathetic. In *Herring*, however, Britten treats these themes with a lightness of touch and an easily satirical manner, in complete contrast with the stark melodrama of *Grimes*, and it has established itself as one of the few British comic operas to endure alongside the work of Gilbert and Sullivan – to which it is more than a little indebted.

Britten turned to his friend Eric Crozier for his libretto, and it is evident from their correspondence that both the characters and the village were based on specific models, though the ultimate source for the opera is a tale by Guy de Maupassant. Small-minded pomposity, malice and sanctimoniousness are personified by the leading players: Lady Billows, the Mayor, the Vicar, the Schoolmistress Miss Wordsworth, Florence Pike, Police Superintendent Budd, and Sid and Nancy. Each plays a hand in the persecution of the eponymous Albert, and the plot – "mummy's boy" Albert Herring is reluctantly nominated for the honour (and £25 cash prize) of May

Queen – is in essence a frame on which to hang Britten and Crozier's hilarious parody of provincial life.

Britten's score intensifies Crozier's caricatures by labelling them with musical quotations. The Vicar, for example, is set to music that fuses the Victorian hymn-tradition and "mummerset" folk song; Miss Wordsworth is lampooned through a pastiche of the very worst British ballads; and Superintendent Budd's bull-doggish Britishness is coloured by a spluttering double-bass theme. As her name suggests, Mrs Billows is the opera's most inflated character and her music veers between the grandiosity of Baroque opera and the banner-waving jingoism associated with Parry and (unfairly) Elgar. Perhaps the most unlikely reference occurs when Sid and Nancy spike Albert's lemonade with rum – this sparks the opera's most chaotic set-piece, in which Britten quotes the love-potion theme from Wagner's *Tristan und Isolde*.

The fleetness of *Albert Herring*, its fizzing ensembles, its chamber orchestration (it's scored for only twelve parts) and its adoption of forms such as keyboard-accompanied recitative are all reminiscent of eighteenth-century opera. In particular, *Herring* recalls Mozart's *Così fan tutte*, a work that Britten acknowledged as his model. The resemblance is especially marked in the final scene, in which Britten joins nine of the characters in a threnody ("In the midst of life is death") sung in response to the the (untrue) news that Albert is dead. Here the tone is distinctly reminiscent of *Così's* bitter-sweet atmosphere, in a finale that reveals *Albert Herring* as a quintessentially English lament for a way of life that is passing away.

Britten's recording of *Herring* is indispensable. His conducting is superb, with an ideal sense of balance and pace. The momentum hardly flags during the two-and-a-half-hour duration, and with a cut-down ECO he achieves an extraordinary range of colour and expression. Drawn from Britten's "Aldeburgh family" of regular collaborators, the cast is uniformly excellent. Peter Pears was too old to have played Albert on stage, but his comic timing and the ease of his tenor voice make him an ideal protagonist on record. Catherine Wilson and Joseph Ward are in superb form as the free spirits Sid and Nancy, and Sylvia Fisher sinks her teeth into the old dragon, Lady Billows, with tremendous vitality.

Benjamin Britten

A Midsummer Night's Dream

Alfred Deller (Oberon), Elizabeth Harwood (Tytania), Peter Pears
(Lysander), Josephine Veasey (Hermia), Heather Harper (Helena); London
Symphony Orchestra; Benjamin Britten (conductor)

London 425 663-2LH2; 2 CDs; full price

Shakespeare has suffered some terrible operatic settings, and yet he has also inspired some of the finest operas ever written. One of these is Britten's adaptation of *A Midsummer Night's Dream*, a project that came into being in 1959, when it became obvious to Britten that there was no time to commission a new libretto for the planned opening of the new concert hall in Aldeburgh the following year. Out of necessity he turned to the greatest of all dramatists, and within just seven months the entire work was complete. Necessity also dictated that half the play be jettisoned, although some new text was added and some lines redistributed as well (Puck's words often find themselves in the mouths of the fairies) – a procedure that met with some disapproval. Britten's response was typically confident: "The original Shakespeare will survive". Despite illness, the composer conducted the first night, having assembled many of his favourite singers – Jennifer Vyvyan as Tytania, Owen Brannigan as Bottom and, of course, Britten's muse and lifetime companion Peter Pears – but this time in the relatively minor role of Flute, notable, chiefly, for its "Mad Scene". Britten scored Oberon for the great English counter-tenor Alfred Deller, and – in a brilliant touch – made the part of Puck a speaking role (it is often played by a dancer) accompanied by raps on a drum and trumpet cadenzas.

Focusing on the opposing worlds of night and day, of waking and sleeping, of the natural and the supernatural, *A Midsummer Night's Dream* is characterized by utterly distinctive and appropriate sound-worlds, as Britten uses his remarkable gift for orchestration to achieve just the right effect for each group of characters. Harps, celesta, percussion and harpsichord are used to accompany the mysterious and sinister world of the fairies; strings and woodwind are associated with the lovers; bassoon and low brass define the bumbling rustics. The vocal score is one of Britten's richest, with the fairies much spikier than might be expected, and Tytania's coloratura and Oberon's counter-tenor sounding suitably other-worldly. Oberon is especially remarkable in that there is a seam of decidedly human malevolence running beneath the surface, and his equivocal character – thought by David Drew to be "a more grimly effective horror than Quint" – allows the performer enormous scope in interpretation. Of the various ensembles, the extraordinarily cocky Act I duet between Lysander and Hermia, "I swear to thee", which moves through twelve major triads before arriving at a gloriously rich C major, and the Act III quartet "And I have found Demetrius", are two of the opera's high points. But, as with *Peter Grimes*, the overall setting and the atmosphere of *A Midsummer Night's Dream* are at least as important as any individual character, and, in the end, it is the extraordinary evocation of the sighing, creaking, rustling forest that is the opera's most memorable feature.

This superb performance of *A Midsummer Night's Dream*, recorded in 1966, is celebrated for the composer's wonderfully vigorous direction of the London Symphony Orchestra, and the extraordinary way in which he manages to highlight the instrumental detail without ever losing sight of the shape and intricacy of the vocal lines. These are particularly well sung by Alfred Deller and Peter Pears, although both were well into their fifties at the time. The rustics are engagingly led by Owen Brannigan as an hilarious Bottom, and the three female leads are ravishingly sung by Elizabeth Harwood, Josephine Veasey and Heather Harper. The sound is bright and the production standards are pretty well faultless.

Pier Francesco Cavalli

La Calisto

Maria Bayo (Calisto), Marcello Lippi (Giove), Graham Pushee (Endymion), Simon Keenlyside ((Mercurio), Alessandra Mantovani (Diana); Concerto Vocale; René Jacobs (conductor)

Harmonia Mundi HMC 901515.17; 3 CDs; full price

By the middle of the seventeenth century the Venetian mania for opera was already at its height, with six opera houses in operation to satisfy public demand. Cavalli, a pupil of Monteverdi, was quick to exploit the situation: in 1639 he signed a contract with the Teatro San Cassiano which committed him to running the company as well as composing for it, a position that must have made him acutely sensitive to the needs of his audience. Cavalli is the first composer to set out to produce an accessible, repeatable operatic formula, and though he's not of the same stature as Monteverdi, his best works have a vitality and a dramatic atmosphere that makes them effortlessly enjoyable.

Though not a success on its premiere, La Calisto is today the only Cavalli opera that's performed with any frequency. Even so, it deserves to be better known: Giovanni Faustini's excellent libretto combines two stories from Ovid's Metamorphoses and turns them into something that at times resembles a Carry On film, with much sexual innuendo, cross-dressing and furtive coupling. In doing this Faustini was simply forcing classical legend, which was no longer very popular on the Venetian stage, into the shape of the comedy of sexual intrigue, which was. Callisto, one of Diana's nymphs, attracts the attention of the lecherous Jove, who disguises himself as Diana in order to win Callisto's favour.

When Jove's infidelity is discovered by his wife, Juno, the Furies turn Callisto into a bear on the order of the wronged wife. Jove confesses his deceit, but promises he will raise Callisto to the stars at her death; the opera ends with Mercury and Callisto celebrating her ascension to the heavens. There's also an amorous subplot, involving Diana, her suitor Endymion, and the jealous Pan.

Cavalli matches his librettist for inventiveness, employing different types of music for different characters: sensual sweetness for Callisto ("the words are sweet but the tune is lewd", is how Mercury describes one of her arias); opulent lyricism for Diana and her lover Endymion, heard at its most beautiful in Endymion's song to the moon, "Lucidissima face"; and punchy arioso recitatives for Pan and his satyrs, which effectively suggest a completely alien culture (analogous to the conventional representation of servants). Much of the dramatic momentum and the wit of the piece is created by changes of pace and switches of musical style. In the scene when the satyrs, having captured Endymion, are threatening to kill him, his plaintive entreaties are met with a lyrical, rustic serenade, "Miserabile", sung by his tormentors – a particularly black piece of irony. The popularity of the love duet with Venetian audiences was such that Jove and Callisto are given two, the first an extraordinarily rhapsodic exchange of short phrases, very close in feeling to the end of Montervedi's *Poppea*.

As in his previous recordings of seventeenth-century opera, René Jacobs has no qualms about filling out the textures with instrumental music by other composers when it seems appropriate. On this recording it works to perfection, and Jacobs reveals *La Calisto* as a dramatic masterpiece. Each separate domain of the opera – the gods, the mortals and the satyrs – is clearly defined, and the casting is strong in every role. As Jove, Marcello Lippi is a tour de force: using his natural voice, a warm baritone, when playing Jove himself, and a comical but not unpleasant falsetto when disguised as Diana. Maria Bayo's Callisto is appropriately languorous and sweet-toned, and Graham Pushee's countertenor Endymion is memorable for the sweetness of tone and evenness of line.

Gustave Charpentier

Louise

Beverly Sills (Louise), Nicolai Gedda (Julien), José van Dam (Father),
Mignon Dunn (Mother); Paris Opéra Chorus and Orchestra; Julius Rudel
(conductor)

EMI CMS5 65299-3; 2 CDs; mid-price

Despite the precedent of Bizet's
Carmen (see p.27) and the example set by the literary endeavours
of Emile Zola and Gustave
Flaubert, the vast majority of
nineteenth-century French opera
composers were content to leave
realism to the Italians. There were
a few exceptions, however, of
which the best known is Gustave
Charpentier's *Louise*, an audacious exploration of the Parisian
demi-monde and an unflinching critique of public hypocrisy.
Charpentier's current obscurity would have been unimaginable
to his peers. While a student at the Paris Conservatoire he was
catapulted to national celebrity after winning the coveted Prix de
Rome, which enabled him to study in Italy. While there he
composed a range of popular pieces, including the first act of
Louise. The full score occupied him for another decade, and by
the time *Louise* made it to the stage of the Opéra-Comique in
1900 it was, musically at least, obsolete. But Charpentier's canny
fusion of lyricism, street songs, vivid characterizations and social
commentary ensured that the work was a hit with Paris's champagne socialists.

Devised by Charpentier, the plot is similar to Puccini's *La
Bohème*, which was written at much the same time, but *Louise*
is set in contemporary Paris, and paints a more accurate pic-
ture of life on the edge of society. Louise is a dressmaker in

love with the poet Julien. They want to marry, but Louise's parents disapprove of the poet and forbid what they believe to be a misalliance. Julien follows her to work, where he persuades her to elope with him. Some time later they are living in bohemian squalor. Louise is happy, but news of her father's illness compels her to return home. Having recovered, he begs his daughter to leave Julien and return to the bourgeois life she left behind. She refuses, and runs from the house, leaving her parents cursing Paris for having taken their daughter away from them.

The style of Charpentier's music is very much of its time and place, owing particular debts to Gounod and Delibes, but his attention to detail, his recreation of the sounds of Parisian street life and his observation of "real life" make it unique among French lyric operas. He even went so far as to demand his cast sing their roles in a Parisian dialect, and the bittersweet, minor-key air that pervades the score has an atmosphere all its own. On the whole the story is told through gentle, illustrative music which doesn't touch the intense heights of Italian *verismo*, and most of the melodies are typical of opéra-comique, with a sweep and charm that you might expect from a pupil of Massenet. Fluid and highly characterful, *Louise* boasts two delightful roles in the title soprano and Julien's high tenor, but the detailed period atmosphere plays an equally important role in making this one of the most beguiling of French operas.

Of the five recordings of *Louise* to have made it onto CD, by far the most beautifully sung is that conducted by the composer in 1935, with Georges Thill and Ninon Vallin (it's on the Nimbus label). However, Charpentier heavily cut the score for recording purposes and so, for all its qualities, it's of interest primarily to those already familiar with the complete work. As an introduction, EMI's 1967 set, with Gedda and Sills as the lovers, is ideal. Gedda's fluent tenor and Sills's effortless coloratura are memorably supported by the Parisian orchestra and chorus, and the French-born van Dam and Dunn bring just the right measure of authenticity to the roles of the parents.

Claude Debussy

Pelléas et Mélisande

George Shirley (Pelléas), Elizabeth Söderström (Mélisande), Donald McIntyre (Golaud), Yvonne Minton (Geneviève); Royal Opera House Chorus and Orchestra; Pierre Boulez (conductor)

Sony SM3K47265; 3 CDs; mid-price

At the close of the nineteenth century, French music writers were in the habit of bewailing that fact that their nation's music was mortgaged to foreigners, notably Wagner. But in 1902, twenty years after the first performance of *Parsifal* (see p.195), Debussy's *Pelléas et Mélisande* was given its premiere, an occasion, according to Romain Rolland, that was "One of the three or four red-letter days in the history of our lyric stage." Offering the first viable alternative to the thundering passions of contemporaneous opera, *Pelléas et Mélisande* is at once the distillation of Romantic yearning and a forebear of modernism.

When Debussy began setting Maurice Maeterlinck's symbolist play to music (he set it virtually word for word) he found it difficult to exorcize the influence of Wagner, and the shadow of *Parsifal* can be detected in Debussy's harmonies and, most obviously, his use of leitmotifs to signal changes in mood. But Debussy radically revised his approach to text-setting, reaching conclusions of extraordinary novelty. Discretion, understatement and subtlety are the key to an opera that has only four fortissimos in its entire three and a quarter hours, and has little by way of traditional melody. Over a shifting tonal palette, marked by complex, centreless harmonies, Debussy's vocal lines carry the text in a long, soft declamation that sets one syllable to one note.

Completely rejecting the conventional lyricism of Italian, French and German opera, Debussy gives absolutely no opportunities for vocal display: the vocal writing in *Pelléas*, like the light but intricate orchestration, is a means of creating mood and atmosphere, rather than a way of expressing character or furthering the action.

In fact "action" is not the appropriate word: hardly anything happens in *Pelléas*, except in the sense that memories happen. "I shall always prefer a subject where, somehow, action is sacrificed to feeling," Debussy once wrote. The fulcrum of the opera is the tragic relationship between Mélisande, her husband Golaud and his half-brother Pelléas. After she loses her ring in a pool of water Golaud begins to suspect her love for Pelléas, and he sends his young son Yniold to spy on the couple. Eventually, Pelléas and Mélisande confess their love, driving Golaud to murder his brother. Mélisande dies in childbirth, after insisting to Golaud that she has done nothing wrong.

For some people, the lack of incident and tight structure makes *Pelléas* an unreal experience – some, indeed, find it catatonically boring. On the other hand, Stravinsky was drawn to the aristocratic sensuality of Debussy's score, and arch-modernist Pierre Boulez has long championed its destabilized sound-world. To begin to appreciate it, you need to jettison as many preconceptions as possible, for immediacy of experience is everything here. In the composer's own words: "When we really listen to music, we hear immediately what we need to hear . . . We must agree that the beauty of a work of art will always remain a mystery . . . We must at all costs preserve this magic."

This is the most convincing, best recorded and most compellingly sung of modern recordings. The clarity, depth and resonance of the Royal Opera House Orchestra is a revelation, and Boulez's fastidious style seems to lay open Debussy's score, highlighting much that earlier performances failed to grasp. Elizabeth Söderström wallows as Mélisande, and George Shirley thrives as a baritonal tenor Pelléas, rich in low voice but sweet and even above the stave. Yvonne Minton gives a rich performance as Geneviève and the remaining cast are more than satisfactory. A thought-provoking, beautifully executed production.

Leo Delibes

Lakmé

Natalie Dessay (Lakmé), Gregory Kunde (Gerald), José van Dam
(Nilakantha), Delphine Haidan (Mallika); Toulouse Capitole Chorus and
Orchestra; Michel Plasson (conductor)

EMI CDS 7243 556569-2; 2 CDs; full price

Friedrich Nietzsche once claimed
that he liked Leo Delibes because
he had "no pretensions to depth",
and Tchaikovsky claimed to prefer his music to that of Brahms
and Wagner. A committed populist and an extremely adroit pas-
ticheur (his music bears the
imprint of Meyerbeer, Gounod,
Bizet, Bellini and countless oth-
ers), Delibes is nowadays known primarily for one ballet,
Coppélia, and one opera, *Lakmé*. First performed in 1883 (the
year in which the French protectorates of Tunisia and Annam
were established), *Lakmé* epitomizes a strand of exoticism that
was a prominent feature of French culture in the latter half of the
nineteenth century. Exactly twenty years earlier Delibes had
assisted at the first production of Bizet's *Pearlfishers*, an orientalist
opera set in a soft-focus Ceylon, and he had also worked as a student on Meyerbeer's grandiose fantasy *L'Africaine*. With *Lakmé*,
the third of a trio of works for the Opéra-Comique, Delibes created a delightful confection that gave his compatriots an alternative to Richard Wagner and his numerous imitators.

The plot is an engagingly absurd melodrama set in India,
around the middle of the nineteenth century. An English officer,
Gérald, falls in love with the beautiful Brahmin priestess Lakmé.
Her father, Nilakantha, sees him spying on his daughter with his
friend Frédéric on holy ground and swears revenge; he later stabs

him during a procession. Lakmé tends the wounded Gérald, who tells her that he is torn between his love for her and loyalty to his regiment. When she realises that Gérald intends to return to the army, Lakmé takes poison and dies.

The score is as thoroughly conservative as the plot, being constructed from separate numbers (including ballets) that are supported by an orchestra that rarely strays from the role of accompanist. Simple, undemanding and elegant, *Lakmé* is distinguished by some famous set-pieces, the best known of which is Act I's sweetly expansive "Flower Duet", a piece that's been used in British Airways' advertising and innumerable movie soundtracks. It's an episode that sounds like the work of an opium-smoking Bellini – indeed, *Lakmé* resembles an Italian bel canto opera as closely as it resembles any French opera. In addition, Gérald's "Fantasie aux divins mensonges" (Fantasy of divine deception) is one of the great French lyric tenor showpieces, and Lakmé's sparkling "Bell Song" reveals the composer's flair for Italianate melody and coloratura effect as well as his sensitive ear for orchestration. *Lakmé's* delicate and rather camp sound-world is all pastel shades, at its most alluring when providing a flutteringly orientalist accompaniment to the dialogue, and if the characters say little of interest, they do say it beautifully.

Remarkably, for an opera so rich with melody, *Lakmé* has not been frequently recorded. By some way the finest performance on CD is the latest to be released, starring the French coloratura soprano Natalie Dessay in the title role. Her voice has an almost baroque purity to it, a quality well suited to this music, and her quintessentially French style – with generous helpings of porta-mento (the sliding between notes) and a magical sense of shape and movement – gives her performance a dimension that's miss-ing in many others. Gregory Kunde's effortless tenor is no less captivating as Gérald, and Delphine Haidan's mezzo provides the necessary weight for Mallika. Thanks to Michel Plasson's tight direction, the cast work together with an ease that's suggestive of a live production, although it was produced entirely in the studio. The Toulouse orchestra and chorus give typically refined support, and the whole is captured in beautifully recorded sound.

Gaetano Donizetti

L'Elisir d'Amore

Joan Sutherland (Adina), Luciano Pavarotti (Nemorino), Dominic Cossa (Belcore), Spiro Malas (Dulcamara); Ambrosian Opera Chorus; English Chamber Orchestra; Richard Bonynge (conductor)

Decca 414 461-2DH2; 2 CDs; full price

Gaetano Donizetti was a famously fast worker: on being told that Rossini had composed *Il Barbiere di Siviglia* in less than two weeks, he is said to have replied, "I have always thought him a lazy fellow." Even by his standards, however, *L'Elisir d'amore* (The Elixir of Love) was a quick job – a single evening's labour, he claimed. According to a friend, Emilia Branca, the composer had been invited to dinner, but failed to show until the meal was nearly over. Branca recalled Donizetti's excuse: "I was on my way . . . when I went past Romani's [his librettist] house. I stopped in to see if he could give me something. In fact, my good friend handed me an entire duet . . . I felt so inspired that, without realising it, I began to read [the verse] already set to music . . . Tonight before going to bed, I'll orchestrate it, tomorrow morning I'll give it to the copyist." Perhaps. But the composer's haste is at no point reflected in the finished score, which is one of the pearls of Italian comic opera. It was the most popular Donizetti opera during his lifetime. After his death in 1848, however, it fell from the repertoire, along with most of the composer's seventy-two other operas, but fifty years later it was revived in New York as a vehicle for the tenor Enrico Caruso, since when it has been kept alive by his various successors, notably Gigli, Bergonzi, Pavarotti and, most recently, Roberto Alagna – who has already recorded the opera three times.

The appeal of *L'Elisir d'Amore* is not difficult to understand. The score overflows with seductive melodies and the libretto is froth of a high order, with some sharp comedy and heartfelt pathos to elevate the farcical narrative. Nemorino loves Adina, so is saddened to see her flirt with Sergeant Belcore. He decides to buy a "love potion" from the quack Doctor Dulcamara. Nemorino drinks deeply from the bottle (the content of which is principally wine), which gives him confidence in his pursuit of Adina. This is shattered when she announces her intention to marry Belcore. Desperate, Nemorino joins Belcore's regiment. As he leaves he is mobbed by the local village girls (who have heard that Nemorino is to inherit a large sum of money) which leads him to believe in the potion. Adina learns of Dulcamara's involvement and wagers her charms against the Doctor's trickery. Adina soon realizes that she loved Nemorino all along, and all ends happily.

Unlike Rossini's operas, which begin much better than they end, *L'Elisir* gets steadily more remarkable and inventive. Nemorino's opening ballad, "Quanto è bella" (How lovely she is), would have sufficed for most of Donizetti's contemporaries as the opera's tenor showpiece, but Donizetti follows it up with a glorious duet with Adina, a sparkling solo arietta and, to cap it all, the mournful aria "Una furtiva lagrima" (One furtive tear) – arguably the most touching episode in all romantic Italian opera. This may be the opera's crowning achievement, but there are many other highlights, famously Adina's challenge to Dulcamara, "Quanto amore" (Such love), and the good Doctor's opening "patter" song.

Recorded in 1969, when he was at the height of his powers, Pavarotti's first recording as Nemorino is a dream performance: his sweet, effortless, and characterful voice makes for intoxicating listening. As always, his partnership with Sutherland is engagingly spontaneous, and her technical brilliance sets the music alight. Dominic Cossa is a swaggering, full-throated Belcore, Spiro Malas is an amiable Dulcamara, and Bonynge conducts with equal measures of verve and sentimentality.

24

Gaetano Donizetti

Lucia di Lammermoor

Montserrat Caballé (Lucia), José Carreras (Edgardo), Vicente Sardinero (Enrico); Ambrosian Opera Chorus; New Philharmonia; Jesus López-Cobos (conductor)

Philips 446 551-2PM2; 2 CDs; mid-price

In the history of opera perhaps no more than a dozen operas have achieved immediate international success and held on to it. *Lucia di Lammermoor* is one of those dozen, even if the reasons for its popularity have changed over the years. During the decade after its first performance in 1835 *Lucia* was hailed as a work of sensational musical theatre. It remained popular after Donizetti's death as an alternative to the weightier experiences being provided by Verdi and his imitators, but as its histrionics began to appear somewhat shallow by comparison with the increasing sophistication of German and French opera so *Lucia* was regarded solely as a star vehicle for lyric tenors and coloratura sopranos. *Lucia* certainly is a star vehicle, but it is also one of the most engrossing Italian operas of the nineteenth century. The extreme musical and theatrical contrasts, and the speed with which the action unfolds, make it a thrillingly immediate experience, while Donizetti's melodies are expressive as well as attractive, and his orchestration – with its bittersweet amplification of the brass – is as ripe as anything before Verdi's *Don Carlo*.

The plot of *Lucia di Lammermoor* is taken (like that of so many other romantic Italian operas) from a novel by Sir Walter Scott – in this case *The Bride of Lammermoor*, which was published in 1819. Set in sixteenth-century Scotland, the story pivots on the machinations of Enrico, who is determined that his sister Lucia should marry Arturo, since the union will strengthen his political situation. But she loves Edgardo, a member of the Ravenswood family and her brother's sworn enemy. Enrico tricks Lucia into marrying Arturo (by forging a letter to prove Edgardo's infidelity) and then challenges Edgardo to a duel. Meanwhile, Lucia murders the hapless Arturo. She appears on stage, covered in blood and carrying a knife, hallucinating that she is about to marry Edgardo, then falls dead to the ground. Hearing of Lucia's death, Edgardo stabs himself.

Lucia di Lammermoor is opera at its most blatantly emotional. The libretto is all primary colours and the characters behave with scant regard for reason, but the power of the music is more than sufficient to overcome these far from uncommon flaws. In particular the title role is littered with unforgettable melodies, and Lucia's duets with Edgardo, her part in the celebrated Act II sextet and the exquisite "mad scene" are highlights of Italian opera. Edgardo's fearsomely demanding tenor role (which calls for an F above high C) is no less tuneful, and in his "Wolf's Crag" duet with the baritone Enrico his role becomes sensationally exciting. Badly performed – and, considering the difficulty of the leading roles, this is not unlikely – *Lucia* can seem little more than tuneful lunacy. When performed well, however, it is irresistible.

The finest available recording was made in 1976 with Jesus López-Cobos conducting an uncut score (the first) and a young Spanish tenor called José Carreras as Edgardo. This is perhaps Carreras's greatest moment on record. The voice is warm and heroic, ringing in its high notes and effortlessly fluent in its delivery. The articulation is typically characterful and his shaping of Donizetti's long phrases – with extended crescendos building to some roof-lifting notes – is truly extraordinary. His Lucia, Montserrat Caballé, is equally thrilling, and while some may find the voice a little shrill in parts, it is a magnificent instrument and she uses it with rare intelligence. Sardiniero is a suitably villainous Enrico, particularly in his pounding "Wolf's Crag" duet with Carreras, and López-Cobos steers the work and the virtuosic New Philharmonia with equal measures of drama and sensitivity.

25

Gaetano Donizetti

La Fille du régiment

Joan Sutherland (Marie), Luciano Pavarotti (Tonio), Spiro Malas (Sulpice),
Monica Sinclair (Marquise); Royal Opera House Chorus and Orchestra;
Richard Bonynge (conductor)

Decca 414 520-2DH2; 2 CDs; full price

Of the five operas Donizetti wrote to a French libretto, by far the most enjoyable is *La Fille du régiment* (The Daughter of the Regiment), a tub-thumping, banner-waving homage to France, and the best French opera not written by a Frenchman. So great was its popularity that there were nearly fifty performances of the first production in 1840, while the Act II chorus "Salut, à la France" was raised to the status of an unofficial anthem. Dozens of new productions followed until the 1870s, when Donizetti's light and florid style fell from fashion. It returned to the repertoire during the first half of the twentieth century as a vehicle for coloratura sopranos, but such are the demands of the tenor lead that new productions are increasingly rare.

The plot is delicious nonsense. Marie has been brought up in a regimental barracks by the amiable Sergeant Sulpice. She has fallen in love with the young captain Tonio, who secretly reciprocates her feelings. Unfortunately, they can never marry since her husband has to be a member of her regiment. Tonio enlists, but their relationship is again threatened by the Marquise de Birkenfeld, who undertakes to introduce Marie to "polite" society, instructing her in etiquette, dancing and conversation. Tonio and the regiment arrive at the Marquise's castle where he confronts her with his petition for Marie's hand. When it is revealed that the Marquise is, in fact, Marie's mother, she agrees to their marriage and all ends happily.

Marie and Tonio are gloriously simple comic characters and Donizetti gave them music of joyful beauty. Of the countless good tunes, Marie's regimental song, "Chacun le sait" (Everyone knows), and her farewell to Tonio, "Il faut partir" (I must go), are particularly fine, but it is Tonio's Act I "Ah mes amis" (Ah, my friends) that is the great tour de force. One night at Covent Garden in 1966 Luciano Pavarotti made himself a superstar with his rendition of this ten-minute burst of riotous fun, in which the tenor is required to execute almost every barnstorming trick in the book – including a finale with nine consecutive high Cs. The overall tone of the orchestral music is militaristic, as you might expect, but it is sardonic stuff, with Donizetti using the marching-band stereotype as a foil to the pretensions of the Marquise's milieu. But as with all of Donizetti's operas, the singing is the thing, and once you've heard the tumbling run of hit songs you might know what Mendelssohn meant when he remarked that he wished he had composed *La Fille du régiment*.

Since World War II only two tenors have had the technique to play Tonio as the composer intended: Alfredo Kraus and Luciano Pavarotti. The latter sang it only a few times but fortunately he recorded the opera a year after his astonishing Covent Garden performance – and it remains his greatest two hours in the studio. Partnered by Joan Sutherland, who sang Marie alongside him at Covent Garden, he strolls through the opera with a unique combination of charm, wit and skill. The breathtaking "Ah mes amis" is perhaps his most stunning moment on disc – he negotiates its fearsome acrobatics as if he were singing the music an octave lower – and his ensembles with Joan Sutherland are the last word in élan. Of Sutherland's performance it's sufficient to say that she tackles the obstacle course of Marie's music with equal fluency. In short, everyone sounds as if they are having a whale of a time, and the recording itself is fresh and immediate.

26

Gaetano Donizetti

Don Pasquale

Fernando Corena (Pasquale), Tom Krause (Malatesta), Graziella Sciutti (Norina), Juan Oncina (Ernesto); Vienna State Opera Chorus and Orchestra; István Kertész (conductor)

Decca 433 036-2DM2; 2 CDs; mid-price

Don Pasquale was written in 1842, six years before the composer's death, and with its light orchestration and delicate vocal writing it seems to hark back – with a hint of autumnal melancholy – to the comic operas of Mozart, suggesting a degree of re-evaluation after many years' devotion to hearty extroversion. However, Donizetti remained true to form in his choice of libretto, a text that lies squarely in the comic tradition of Rossini.

The wealthy and childless bachelor Don Pasquale wishes to disinherit his troublesome nephew Ernesto, who is in love with the widow Norina. Pasquale asks Dr Malatesta to find him a wife to whom he can leave his fortune. Malatesta is a friend to both uncle and nephew, and sets Don Pasquale up with "Sofronia" – Norina in disguise. Sofronia and Pasquale marry, whereupon she begins to make his life a misery, spending ever larger amounts of his money. When Pasquale learns that Sofronia has arranged to meet a stranger, he and Malatesta prepare to catch the adulterers red-handed. Sofronia and Ernesto are duly discovered. Pasquale is angry that he has been made to look a fool, but so delighted is he to discover that his marriage is a sham that he readily blesses his nephew's marriage to Norina.

Don Pasquale is a quick-witted, rapidly paced opera – a series of amusing situations in which episodes of knockabout humour are swiftly tempered by pathos, and vice versa. The third act provides a good example, when Norina, having slapped Don Pasquale during their quarrel over her intended visit to the theatre, expresses her remorse at having driven the old fool to such despair; the sudden explosion of energy that follows, brought about by the exasperated Don's discovery that his wife is to meet another man, is typical of the composer's habit of quickly changing the emotional temperature. The swiftness of pace is enhanced by the use of string-accompanied recitative, and a vocal score largely made up of rapid character-arias such as Norina's lively "So anch'io la virtù magica" (I know what spells a glance can dart). But Donizetti still takes the time to indulge his passion for bel canto, generating a melodic richness that culminates in Ernesto's exquisite tenor cantilena "Com è gentil" (How gentle), and his idyllic duet with Norina, "Tornami a dir" (Return to me). Tradition has it that "Com è gentil" was a last-minute addition: Donizetti allegedly took it from a box of miscellaneous music and sent it to Giovanni Mario, the tenor in the first performance, advising him to use it for his serenade to Norina. It was an immediate sensation, and barrel-organists all over Italy added it to their repertoire within a week of the premiere.

The Piccola Scala staged a famous production of *Don Pasquale* in 1959, building it round the talents of Graziella Sciutti. Decca recorded her in the role of Norina not long after and her performance set the bennchmark – her voice is light, brilliantly flexible and shimmering with personality. Similarly convincing is Fernando Corena as Pasquale, and Tom Krause gives a nicely judged portrayal of Malatesta. István Kertész, in one of his few operatic recordings, strongly suggests he should have made more, particularly in his handling of the ensemble pieces. The orchestra is of a refinement that Donizetti would never have expected, but this is all to the good. Also included is a recording of Cimarosa's brilliantly witty *Il maestro di cappella* (The Chapel Master), a monologue for a conductor attempting to rehearse his lousy orchestra in impossible conditions.

27

John Gay

The Beggar's Opera

Sarah Walker (Mrs Peachum/Mrs Trapes), Anne Dawson (Lucy), Adrian Thompson (Macheath), Bronwen Mills (Polly), Bob Hoskins (Beggar); Broadside Band; Jeremy Barlow (conductor)

Hyperion CDA 66591; 2 CDs; full price

England's hopes of an operatic culture that was independent of mainland Europe died with Henry Purcell. However, English enthusiasm for Italian opera at the end of the seventeenth century and the beginning of the eighteenth produced a not untypical reaction: unable to compete with the skill of Italian composers, the English resorted to ridicule and created a satirical genre known as "ballad opera". The one surviving example of this bastard form is John Gay's *Beggar's Opera*. Musical talent was not one of Gay's accomplishments: he created the ballad opera by piecing together some popular tunes (including music from his friend Handel's *Rinaldo*), engaging the composer John Pepusch to provide a structure and overtures, and then threading the whole thing together with his own comic dialogue. Not even the idea was Gay's. It is said to have come from Jonathan Swift who, in 1715, wrote to Gay that "a Newgate Pastoral might make an odd, pretty sort of thing". When, in 1724, the highwayman Jack Shepherd was hanged at Newgate prison, and the crook who had informed against him was stabbed to death in court, Gay found the material he needed for his patchwork creation.

The plot concerns the lovable rogue Macheath, a highwayman who seduces Polly, daughter of the criminal Peachum, and Lucy, daughter of the jailer Lockit. He is arrested in his favourite bordello and taken to Newgate prison, where Lucy and Polly compete with one another for Macheath's affections. To make matters worse, four women (each carrying a child by Macheath) step forward, at which point the Highwayman exclaims, "This is too much!" The Beggar of the title then steps forward, pardons Macheath and unites him with Polly.

The broad and essentially English satire of *The Beggar's Opera* has many targets, including the fashionable opera of the day, visiting Italian personalities such as the rival prima donnas Faustina and Cuzzoni (satirized in the rivalry of Polly and Lucy), and figures of authority, such as the Prime Minister Sir Robert Walpole. The force of some of this ridicule has of course been lost as its victims recede into history, but Gay's subversive wit still packs a punch in the modern world, as demonstrated by Kurt Weill's *Die Dreigroschenoper* (see p.199), an adaptation of *The Beggar's Opera* produced two centuries later. *The Beggar's Opera* is one of the funniest entertainments ever created for the English stage, with much of the humour deriving from the honesty and directness with which the low-life world is depicted, and the way criminality is presented as having its own skewed morality. Most modern productions of *The Beggar's Opera* treat it as a romp in fancy dress, but even with its happy ending (in itself ridiculing the convention), it is a profoundly cynical work which suggests that most people are motivated by greed and selfishness and that everybody has a price. The work's nihilism is oddly undepressing, however, largely because of the sheer panache with which Gay's characters pursue their wickedness.

Jeremy Barlow's arrangement of *The Beggar's Opera* is by some way the finest on record: his instrumental accompaniments are simple and broadly eighteenth century in style; he directs the work with passion and wit; and the cast is ideal. Bob Hoskins's Beggar is overacted enough to compensate for the lack of visual stimulus, while Sarah Walker's Mrs Peachum is all bloomers and indignation, leaving Adrian Thompson's Macheath almost overawed. Unlike some, Barlow leaves Gay's text unedited, which is reasonable since the songs are almost meaningless without the intervening dialogue, and the spoken episodes do nothing to disrupt this energetic production.

28

George Gershwin

Porgy and Bess

Willard White (Porgy), Cynthia Haymon (Bess), Harolyn Blackwell (Clara), Damon Evans (Sportin' Life); Glyndebourne Festival Chorus; London Philharmonic Orchestra; Simon Rattle (conductor)

EMI CDS7 49568-2; 3 CDs; full price

George Gershwin's professional life began on Tin Pan Alley, where he worked plugging other composers' songs. By 1919 he was writing his own material, and in that year he had his first hit, 'Swanee', from his comedy *La La Lucille*. Tremendous success soon followed, with songs such as "Fascinatin' Rhythm" and "Lady Be Good", yet Gershwin was never entirely satisfied with his lot. Fascinated since childhood by classical music, he began to consider writing for the concert hall as well for the musical theatre, and after the enormous acclaim for *Rhapsody in Blue* (1924) he gained enough confidence to contemplate creating a full-length opera. A decade passed, however, before he finally chose his subject, the black ghettos of South Carolina, taking as his source DuBose and Dorothy Heyward's 1926 novel *Porgy*.

The Heywards clung to the basic plot of their novel for the libretto. The pugnacious stevedore Crown and the crippled Porgy vie for the affections of the fickle Bess. She vacillates between the two, until Porgy is provoked into killing his rival. While Porgy is identifying the body for the police, Bess is lured away to New York by the dealer Sportin' Life. When Porgy returns to find Bess gone, he sets out on the journey to find her.

Gershwin conceived *Porgy and Bess* as a fusion of classical and popular music, a reconciliation of the structural demands of through-composed opera with the populist forms of the musical. But although his achievement of this goal is now acknowledged on both sides of the musical divide (due in part to landmark productions at the Met and Glyndebourne in the 1980s), *Porgy and Bess* didn't initially achieve the respect it's due. While jazz fans were dismissive of his use of Afro-American music, opera critics sniffily complained that Gershwin's "opera" was basically just a string of hit tunes. Gershwin responded to the latter charge by pointing out that "nearly all of Verdi's operas contain what are known as 'song hits'", and he might have gone on to point out that very few twentieth-century composers of any type have written songs as tuneful and powerful as "Summertime", "I Got Plenty o' Nuttin'", "Bess, You Is My Woman" and "It Ain't Necessarily So". He might have been pitching it a bit high when he said his masterwork would "resemble a combination of the drama and romance of *Carmen* and the beauty of *Meistersinger*", but *Porgy and Bess* is emphatically a true opera: its music is continuous, its score is rigorously structured and threaded with leit-motifs, and the highly developed melodies call for a classical singing technique – especially Porgy, whose role is frequently cut to lessen the strain. Achieving a feeling of authenticity not through cheap stunts but primarily through "blue note" harmony and syncopated rhythm (the only orchestral effects are a banjo and African drums), Gershwin created what remains opera's only successful treatment of African-American experience.

Simon Rattle's classic 1988 recording of the opera followed Glyndebourne's much-praised production. The cast, chorus and orchestra are the same as appeared on stage, and this brings a real integrity to the performance, which is dominated by the authoritative portrayal of Porgy by Willard White, whose association with the role spans more than twenty years and, to date, three recordings. Cynthia Haymon's Bess is instantly likable, and she gives an unforgettably sensual performance of "Summertime", while the difficult role of Sportin' Life is energetically carried by the tenor Damon Evans. Rattle audibly enjoys himself throughout, and the London Philharmonic Orchestra come remarkably close to capturing the bluesy, improvisational character of Gershwin's score.

Umberto Giordano

Andrea Chénier

Franco Corelli (Chénier), Antonietta Stella (Maddalena de Coigny), Mario Sereni (Gérard); Rome Opera Chorus and Orchestra; Gabriele Santini (conductor)

EMI CMS5 65287-2; 2 CDs; mid-price

The typical *verismo* opera was about simple, decidedly unpoetic characters in grubby, true-to-life situations, and lasted a somewhat shorter time than a soccer game. Perhaps the finest exception to these rules is Umberto Giordano's remarkable portrayal of the last five years in the life of the French Revolutionary poet André Chénier. Composed between 1894 and 1896, *Andrea Chénier* was first performed five weeks after Puccini's *La Bohème* – which accounts for its failure to make its mark as rapidly as should have been the case – and has remained the composer's best-known work.

Giordano's attraction to Chénier can perhaps be traced to his own divided ambitions as a young man, when, like his hero, he was torn between a life in the army and art. He chose the latter in defiance of his family's wishes, and lived a bohemian existence during the early 1890s until, in 1894, he secured use of a libretto by Puccini's hugely successful librettist Luigi Illica, and began composing *Andrea Chénier*. Set during the years of the Terror, the opera's story is set in motion by Chénier's love for the beautiful, socially conscious aristocrat, Maddalena de Coigny. Gérard, a former friend of Chénier's now working for Robespierre, begins spying on him and Maddalena. Chénier is eventually arrested for treason; Gérard signs the indictment and Chénier is sentenced to death. In the city prison Gérard allows Maddalena to replace another female inmate, and she joins Chénier at the guillotine.

Illica's libretto makes liberal use of Chénier's poetry, and Giordano's music is ideally suited to the high-flown verse. The score is peppered with French revolutionary songs and anthems, including a glorious transcription of *La Marseillaise*, but like *Bohème*, *Tosca*, *Butterfly* and *Turandot*, it is for its set-pieces, most of which are dominated by the title role's fearsomely demanding heroic tenor, that *Andrea Chénier* stands out. Unlike Puccini, however, there is an artless sincerity to Giordano's hand-wringing. Indeed, Puccini was too calculating an artist to risk anything as ingenuously affirmative as the prison finale, an absurdly upbeat ending in which the lovers sing in gushing unison while being transported in a tumbrel to their deaths, or the court scenes, in which Chénier conducts himself in a manner that suggests a failure to grasp the gravity of the situation. Yet such is the splendour of Giordano's music – famously the tenor's monologue "Un dì all'azzuro spazio" (I gazed one day), Gérard's "Nemico della patria" (Enemy of his country) and the concluding dam-buster duet "Vicino a te" (Beside you) – that you're unlikely to trouble yourself over such technicalities as plausibility.

Fortunately, the finest post-war Chénier recorded the role in his prime. Franco Corelli sounds at times a little too pleased with himself, but he had a lot to be pleased about – his performance is a masterclass in romantic tenor singing. Finding the range no problem, he sails through even the most taxing scenes, and the massive, open-throated warmth of his voice brings Chénier's verse to life like no other singer before or since. Antonietta Stella is sometimes a little out of her depth as Maddalena, but she sings her show-stopper "La mamma morta" (a number made famous by the film *Philadelphia*) with her heart on her sleeve, and her contribution to the final duet is outstanding. Mario Sereni is 100 percent ham, and this is entirely to his advantage as Gérard. Santini is too generous a conductor, allowing his leads a freedom that can lead to a loss of tension, but the orchestra plays superbly, and the whole is captured in magnificent sound.

30

Philip Glass

Akhnaten

Paul Esswood (Akhnaten), Milagr Vargas (Nefertiti); Stuttgart Opera Chorus and Orchestra; Russell Davies (conductor)

Sony M2K42457; 2 CDs; full price

Philip Glass is one of the few living composers to have circumvented the dead-end obscurities of the contemporary avant-garde and successfully reinvented operatic style for a new generation. The radical simplicity of his Minimalist style, which is characterized above all by the repetition of small, cell-like phrases over long periods of time, imbues his music with a powerful sense of suspended time, and his operas unfold slowly, as patterns gradually grow and contract in restless development. Though often open to the accusation of being shallow and uneventful, Glass's music is unmistakably his, and at its best it's insidiously effective.

Akhnaten (1984) is the third part of a trilogy of philosophico-historical operas that began with two highly experimental stage works: *Einstein on the Beach* and *Satyagraha*, a piece centred on the life of Gandhi. The inspiration for *Akhnaten* came primarily from Sigmund Freud's *Moses and Monotheism* and Immanuel Velikovsky's *Oedipus and Akhnaten*. The latter was particularly important in determining his approach to the opera, for in it Velikovsky attempted to trace the Oedipus myth and the "mother complex" back to the life of the Egyptian pharaoh Akhnaten. Furthermore, though Akhnaten's revolutionary monotheism was replaced by the old theology as soon as he was dead, Velikovsky argued that the Judeo-Christian belief system could ultimately be traced back to the pharaoh's doomed enterprise. Akhnaten thus became a figure whose life altered the world as radically as had the physics of Einstein and the politico-philosophical beliefs of Gandhi.

The libretto, written in part by the composer, concentrates on Akhnaten's relationship with Nefertiti, for whom he abandons polygamy, and with whom he builds a city in honour of his new god – the omnipotent Aten. Although his people suffer hunger and deprivation, and despite his failure to produce a male heir, Akhnaten continues to believe in Aten. His family do not share his faith, and leave him alone in his city, which is destroyed by priests of the old, polytheistic religion. The final scene shifts to the present day, where tourists pick over the ruins of the old city. As they leave it becomes clear that the pharaoh's spirit still lingers.

Akhnaten is a thoroughly modern work, but the libretto makes liberal use of ancient languages – Egyptian, Akkadian and Hebrew – each of which is translated on stage by a narrator. This might suggest a certain theatrical detachment, but *Akhnaten* is an absorbing work of great beauty and considerable lyricism. In particular, Glass's writing for the pharaoh (a counter-tenor), is hypnotic stuff and in his Act II duet with Nefertiti the composer touched a vein of ardent song not normally associated with the aesthetics of Minimalism. Glass also shows himself to be an adroit orchestral colourist, notably in the atmospheric evocation of his court and its rituals, and the orchestra is very much the opera's dominant role. Leitmotif-like themes herald the main characters and events, and the principal characters have distinctly delineated roles within a straightforward linear narrative. This is, in short, a more mainstream opera than anything previously attempted by Glass, so if you're approaching him, and Minimalism, for the first time, this is an excellent place to start.

Russell Davies here conducts many of the original cast from the Stuttgart premiere of *Akhnaten*. Paul Esswood is haunting in the title role, and the remaining players are all exceptionally well cast, giving characterful portrayals. However, *Akhnaten* is an opera in which the orchestra provides the leading voice and the Stuttgart players rise to the occasion – all of which is beautifully captured in an atmospheric recording.

31

Christoph Willibald Gluck

Orfeo ed Euridice

Derek Lee Ragin (Orfeo), Sylvia McNair (Euridice), Cynthia Sieden (Amore); Monteverdi Choir; English Baroque Soloists; John Eliot Gardiner (conductor)

Philips 434 093-2PH2; 2 CDs; full price

With the work of Gluck a new emphasis on emotional truth was introduced into the world of opera. Central to Gluck's artistic credo was the idea that opera should be more organic – that the arias, recitatives, ensembles and choruses should all move the drama forward, instead of being a preordained array of components around which the opera should be constructed. The most popular of Gluck's operas is *Orfeo ed Euridice* (Orpheus and Eurydice), a setting of a tale that has been used by many composers, from Monteverdi via Offenbach to Harrison Birtwistle.

A comparison between the opening of Gluck's treatment of the myth and Monteverdi's treatment of it perfectly illustrates how much opera had changed in the intervening century and a half. Where Monteverdi's hero informs the audience of his unhappiness at Eurydice's death, and the orchestra verifies his emotions through a poignant accompaniment, Gluck dramatizes Orpheus's condition: his heart-rending cries of "Euridice" punctuate a funereal lament sung by a chorus of nymphs surrounding Eurydice's tomb, a passage which leads into the transformation of the hero's misery into an exquisite song of resignation. The tale is the same, but Gluck's music presents a more fully realized mental state, in which emotions are complex and variable.

The eruptions of emotion that occur throughout *Orfeo* gain potency from the poise with which they are expressed. Denuded of all ornament, Gluck's vocal writing possesses a simple beauty that reaches its highest pitch in Orpheus's "Che faro senza Euridice?" (What shall I do without Eurydice?), an outpouring of grief comparable to the closing lament of Purcell's *Dido and Aeneas* (see p.130). With the help of his librettist Calzabigi, Gluck also refined his recitative, making greater dramatic use of a convention that previously had too often dragged the action to a standstill. The fluency of *Orfeo's* recitative, the careful placement of the sumptuously scored choruses and the sparkling interludes (notably the "Dance of the Furies") reveal an exceptional theatrical imagination which, together with Gluck's distinctive gift for expressive melody, contributes much to the sense of cohesion that is *Orfeo's* hallmark. *Orfeo* is Gluck's most exhilarating work, and the joy with which he immersed himself in the poetry of his librettist, Calzabigi, is mirrored throughout the score. As the composer wrote many years later: "If my music has had some success, I think it is my duty to recognise that I am beholden for it to him . . . However much talent a composer may have, he will never produce any but mediocre music if the poet does not awaken in him that enthusiasm without which the productions of all the arts are but feeble and drooping."

Gluck composed the opera twice: in 1762 for Vienna (in Italian) and again in 1774 for Paris (in French). The two editions are very different (the title role of the French version, for example, is greatly expanded and scored for a soprano), but the Italian version is the one you're likeliest to come across. John Eliot Gardiner's recording of the first *Orfeo* (he's also produced a French version) features Derek Lee Ragin's eloquent counter-tenor and Sylvia McNair's soprano, an ideal couple. McNair has established herself as one of the outstanding talents of our time, and although her repertoire now encompasses a large body of nineteenth- and twentieth-century music (see *The Rake's Progress*, p.159), she made her reputation singing earlier repertoire, such as this *Orfeo* – in which she makes an unforgettably moving Euridice. Gardiner is an ever vivid presence; his tempi are fast and he exaggerates throughout, but the performance is generally light, flexible and gripping.

32

Christoph Willibald Gluck

Iphigénie en Tauride

Diana Montague (Iphigénie), John Aler (Pylade), Thomas Allen (Oreste);
Monteverdi Choir; Lyon Opera Orchestra; John Eliot Gardiner (conductor)

Philips 416 148-2PH2; 2 CDs; full price

Gluck's collaboration with the poet Raniero Calzabigi brought about a radical change of direction for opera, as typified by *Orfeo ed Euridice*, a work whose dramatic orchestration and overall sense of momentum were enthrallingly original. The finest libretto that Gluck ever set, however, was by Nicholas-François Guillard, and their collaboration on *Iphigénie en Tauride* (Iphigenia on Tauris) comes as close as possible to the complete realization of the composer's ideals. More sensual, expressive and taut than any other Gluck creation, it was adored by Berlioz and by Richard Strauss – the latter went so far as to prepare a performing edition in which he "modernized" some of the harmony, changed the finales of the first and last acts and introduced ballet music from *Orfeo* and *Armide*. The creation of *Iphigénie en Tauride* provided the fulcrum for one of the most famous rivalries in operatic history, when the director of the Paris Opéra tried to whip up business by arranging for both Gluck and his rival Niccolò Piccini to write an opera based on Euripides' play *Iphigenia on Tauris*. Gluck's work was both superior and more popular, and signalled the eclipse of the old guard, as represented by Piccini.

The drama is set on the island of Tauris, shortly after the Trojan War. Iphigenia (Iphigénie) has become a priestess of Diana and is unaware of her father's murder by her mother and the revenge taken by her brother Orestes (Oreste). Orestes, together with his companion Pylades (Pylade), arrives on the island in disguise. They are captured and the Scythian king, Thoas, orders them to be sacrificed. Still disguised, Orestes tells Iphigenia that her parents and Orestes are all dead. Pursued by the Furies, Orestes persuades her to save Pylades, and just as the sacrifice is about to take place the siblings recognize each other. Diana then appears with a pardon for Orestes.

The opening of *Tauride* is one of Gluck's most wondrous innovations: there is no overture but rather a brief scene-setting prelude, evoking a rising storm, out of which grows the voice of Iphigenia and the commencement of the first scene. This dramatic seamlessness, typical of the entire piece, must have left contemporary audiences dazzled. Gluck's application of instrumentation as a psychological device is as remarkable as the opera's structural perfection. Perhaps the best-known example comes during Act II, when Gluck uses trombones to signify the Furies and then, in a remarkable twist, introduces throbbing semiquavers on one note, stressed every first beat, to indicate that Orestes might never free himself from guilt. But of course the orchestra is used for more than local effect: the score is, in fact, almost symphonic in its richness, and the shifts between recitative, aria and chorus are eased by a stream of constantly inventive instrumental music. With its sense of unstoppable motion, *Iphigénie en Tauride* is the Gluck opera that most closely prefigures the masterworks of the nineteenth century.

John Eliot Gardiner's recording of *Tauride* is one of his finest achievements. His grasp of the score's architecture, the tensile strength of his tempi and the vivid punctuation of his rhythms make this as headily theatrical as any Gluck opera recording. His customary attention to detail, heightening instrumental clarity to a point just short of pedantry, gives the orchestral counterpoint unprecedented power. The cast respond well to Gardiner's direction, and the momentum of the ensemble is consistently impressive – though the voices are rather light, with the exception of Thomas Allen's Orestes. Perfect sound, and a good booklet too.

33

Charles Gounod

Faust

Nicolai Gedda (Faust), Victoria de los Angeles (Marguérite), Boris Christoff (Méphistophélès); Paris Opéra Chorus and Orchestra; André Cluytens (conductor)

EMI CMS7 69983-2; 3 CDs; mid-price

During the first half of the nineteenth century Paris was the centre of European opera, but it was foreign rather than native talent that sustained the scene. Around the middle of the century, however, a Frenchman came close to monopolizing the enthusiasm of the Paris audiences – Charles Gounod. Although he amassed a huge catalogue of music, Gounod was celebrated during his life and is remembered now for just one work: *Faust*. Four years after the 1859 premiere, an English critic complained, "Faust, Faust, Faust, nothing but Faust. Faust on Saturday, Wednesday and Thursday; to be repeated tonight, and on every night until further notice." It is still the most popular French opera ever written, having been played in more than fifty countries and translated into more than twenty-five languages.

As a young man Gounod had been determined to take holy orders, but he was encouraged to pursue his musical talents by the soprano Pauline Viardot, with whom he had a brief affair. The twin inspirations of religion and sex remained constant for most of his life, but nowhere are the sacred and profane more perfectly fused than in his reworking of the Faust myth. Gounod's *Faust* brings you lust, love, hope, despair, religious faith, the supernatural and the cosmic battle between good and evil, all wrapped in music that sticks in the head for months after a single hearing. Indeed, Parisian publishers and organ-grinders capitalized on the opera's catchy melodies so quickly that Gounod is said to have remarked after an early performance of the opera: "I knew I'd heard those tunes before."

The plot broadly follows the first part of Goethe's massive philosophical poem, but abandons most of the philosophy en route. A despairing and lonely Faust raises the Devil who, agreeing to satisfy his sensual desires, conjures the image of beauty and chastity that is Marguérite. With the Devil's help Faust seduces Marguérite, impregnating her with a child, whom, driven to madness, she kills. She is visited in prison by Faust. Rejecting his advances, she prays to God for forgiveness and falls dead to the ground. As Faust is dragged to Hell, Marguérite's soul rises to Heaven.

The Devil certainly has all the best tunes here: all horns and scarlet tights, Gounod's Méphistophélès is a roaring, jubilant portrayal of music-hall wickedness, revelling in a cynicism that brings a genuine darkness to what is otherwise a sophisticatedly depthless opera. The lyrical sweetness of Faust's tenor role suggests little of the turmoil conjured by Goethe – but having said that, his music is glorious, and the love duets and arias, notably Faust's elegiac "Salut, demeure et chaste et pure" (Hail, innocent and pure dwelling) are unforgettable. Marguérite, the weakest of the trio, is an implausible lust object, embodying a sickly sweet Christianity that is all smells and bells, but Gounod observes the operatic protocol by giving her some coloratura showpieces and a part in the opera's thumping trio finale.

Such a sentimental opera demands a conductor with a cast-iron grip if the thing is not to appear completely silly. André Cluytens was that man. He first recorded the opera, in mono, in 1953, with Christoff, Gedda and de los Angeles; he re-recorded it in stereo five years later, and this set is still the benchmark recording. Gedda's tenor was by no means the most beautiful, but he used it with great sensitivity and intelligence. Conversely, de los Angeles's soprano was almost hypnotically sweet, and ideally suited to Marguérite's character, just as Christoff's growling bass perfectly captured the spirit of Gounod's Devil.

34

Georg Frideric Handel

Giulio Cesare

Jennifer Larmore (Giulio Cesare), Barbara Schlick (Cleopatra), Derek Lee Ragin (Tolomeo), Marianne Rørholm (Sesto); Cologne Concerto; René Jacobs (conductor)

Harmonia Mundi HMC 90 1385-7; 4 CDs; full price

Held by many to be the finest of all Handel's operas, and the one that's most frequently performed nowadays, *Giulio Cesare* (Julius Caesar) is also one of his most lavish creations. On record it lasts just under three and a half hours, and the original production – complete with on-stage fireworks, magic-lantern projections and the flamboyant presence of star soprano Francesca Cuzzoni (one of the targets of Gay's *The Beggar's Opera*) – would have lasted even longer than Wagner's *Parsifal*. Drawn from a variety of sources (chiefly a text by Francesco Bussani that had already been used by another composer), Nicola Francesco Haym's libretto is immensely complicated yet retains its dramatic cohesion to a greater extent than anything Handel had previously set – a fact for which the composer should probably take a lot of credit, as the libretto was almost certainly written with his involvement.

The opera is set in Egypt, where Caesar, having defeated Pompey in battle, is presented with the severed head of his rival by Ptolemy (Tolomeo), the joint ruler of Egypt. Cornelia, Pompey's widow, vows to avenge the death of her husband, but her son Sextus (Sesto) takes it upon himself to avenge his father's death. Cleopatra, as appalled as Caesar by the murder of Pompey, allies herself with Caesar against Ptolemy, her brother, while Achilla – a captain in the Egyptian army – promises Ptolemy that he will kill Caesar if as a reward he can marry Cornelia. When Ptolemy reneges on his promise by taking Cornelia for himself, Achilla swaps sides: the final result is the death of Ptolemy and amity between Cleopatra, her lover Caesar, Sextus and Cornelia.

Handel's music matches the drama's scale, but principal amongst this opera's qualities is its concentration on solo arias – Cleopatra and Caesar have eight each. The role of Cleopatra is one of Handel's greatest creations for the female voice, and her Act II recitative and aria "Se pietà di me non sento" (If you feel no pity for me), in which she laments her fate, yearns for revenge and longs for the love of Caesar, is especially wonderful – with a melody of effortless conviction, this is the opera's most emotive episode. The accompanied recitatives are significant for their startling number of modulations, while the vocal lines themselves are both longer and more complex than in any of Handel's previous operas. The score is also notable for a series of powerfully dramatic interludes (such as the clamorous "Battle Symphony" at the beginning of Act III, evoking the conflict between Achilla and Ptolemy's supporters) and some strikingly inventive orchestration – notably Caesar's Act I "Va tacito e nascosto" (Silently and stealthily), a powerful aria in which the text's hunting similes are accompanied by a potent horn obbligato. The title role is weakly defined by Haym's text, however, and it is left entirely to the music to bring Caesar's idealized nobility and courage to life.

Basing his studies on Handel's 1724 edition of the opera, René Jacobs has got rid of inaccuracies perpetuated by later editions, and his faithful attention to Handel's vocal specifications has resulted in a fitting balance of voices in this beautifully recorded performance. As Caesar Jennifer Larmore is a powerful, heroic presence and engagingly resourceful in her mastery of the role's pyrotechnics. Barbara Schlick is sensitive as Cleopatra and Derek Lee Ragin is an enjoyably ominous counter-tenor Ptolemy, reaching stratospheric heights without strain. Jacobs' fluid attention to line avoids the ear-flinching harshness common to many "authentic" conductors – indeed, the recording's great theatricality stems largely from his expressively relaxed approach.

35

George Frideric Handel

Ariodante

Anne Sofie von Otter (Ariodante), Lynne Dawson (Ginevra), Ewa Podles
(Polinesso), Verónica Cangemi (Dalinda); Choeur et Musiciens du Louvre;
Marc Minkowski (conductor)

Archiv 457 271-2; 3 CDs; full price

In 1728 Handel's opera company
collapsed, the death blow having
been dealt by John Gay, whose
Beggar's Opera (see p.53) torpe-
doed traditional Italianate opera
in England. Two years later
Handel resolved to have another
go, making a fresh start at the
King's Theatre. But business was
slow, his new works were unpop-
ular, and the rival Opera of the Nobility scored a major coup by
hiring the legendary castrato Farinelli for his London debut.
Handel responded by moving to Covent Garden, where he
engaged the dancer Maria Sallé for a lavish production of his latest opera *Ariodante*. Its success marked a reversal of fortune for
the composer, albeit a temporary one.

For his libretto Handel turned to an existing text, by Antonio
Salvi, based on Lodovico Ariosto's immense poetic romance
Orlando Furioso (also the source for Lully's *Armide* – see p.87).
The drama unfolds in the palace of the King of Scotland, where
Ariodante and Ginevra are celebrating their engagement.
However, Ariodante has a rival in Polinesso, the Duke of Albany.
Polinesso uses the maid Dalinda to help him falsify evidence of
Ginevra's infidelity. When this is presented to the court, together
with news that Ariodante has thrown himself to his death,
Ginevra goes mad. Ginevra is saved when the dying Polinesso
confesses his plot and Ariodante returns, having faked his suicide.

Ariodante's most striking quality is that both Ariodante and Polinesso are travesti roles – ie, male roles played by women. This means that, with the exception of the King and the two minor roles of Lurcanio and Odoardo, Handel scored all the opera's leads as sopranos. Consequently, most of the duets and ensembles involve the heady union of female voices, a combination that is particularly exquisite in the duets between Ariodante and Ginevra, such as Act I's soaring "Prendi da questa mano" (Take from this hand), in which the lovers pledge their devotion. Ariodante's "masculine" qualities are expressed through some of the composer's most intricate coloratura, but it is Ginevra, rather than Ariodante, who provides the opera's fulcrum. A more rounded personality, she undergoes an emotional transformation from happy innocence to resignation – as expressed through the haunting "Il mio crudel martoro" (My cruel torment), in which she prays for death. The other characters are hardly developed, and Handel devoted rather more attention to the lavish accompaniments, instrumental movements (including a moving depiction of the moon rising over the castle in Act II), dances and choruses, which are superbly integrated into the drama. Each of the acts ends with a ballet, but these are cunningly integrated into the action. In Acts I and III, for example, they are presented as court entertainments, to be enjoyed by the cast as well as the audience, but they were really little more than opportunities for Handel to show off – which he does with irresistible skill. The last scene is the most daring, with a ballet in which Ginevra's good and bad dreams are fully acted out.

Marc Minkowski's recording of *Ariodante* is exceptional, first and foremost, for its casting. The partnership of Anne Sofie von Otter in the title role and Lynne Dawson as Ginevra is intoxicating, and their duets are highlights of modern Baroque recording. The beauty of their voices is intoxicating but both pay acute attention to their diction, and articulate their feelings, as well as their words, with wonderful commitment. The supporting cast and chorus are excellent, and Minkowski's small but resonant orchestra creates a generous background for the vocal score. Minkowski is in typically inventive form, revealing, yet again, his uniquely romantic flair for Baroque music.

Engelbert Humperdinck

Hänsel und Gretel

Anna Moffo (Hänsel), Helen Donath (Gretel), Christa Ludwig (Witch),
Dietrich Fischer-Dieskau (Father), Arleen Augér (Sandman), Lucia Popp
(Dew Fairy); Tolz Boys Choir; Munich Radio Orchestra; Kurt Eichorn (conductor)

RCA 74321 252781-2; 2 CDs; mid-price

Engelbert Humperdinck was one
of the few German composers to
make a name for himself in the
years immediately after Wagner's
death in 1883. This success came
chiefly from one opera, and was
partly attributable to to his decision to do something different
from the work of most of his contemporaries, who tended to pro-
duce mythological dramas in the Wagnerian mode.
Humperdinck had been a friend and colleague of Wagner, but
for his first opera, *Hänsel und Gretel*, Humperdinck turned to the
world of Märchenoper (fairy-tale opera), a style typified by
Weber's *Der Freischütz* (see p.197). The stimulus for turning the
Grimm story into an opera came from Humperdinck's sister,
Adelheid Wette, who in 1890 commissioned him to write the
music for her stage adaptation of it. Though he provided only
four songs, the project led him to write a full-scale opera, which
he completed three years later. His friend Richard Strauss agreed
to conduct the first performance in Weimar, and it made a fortune for the composer and for the theatre. Within twelve months
of the premiere, Humperdinck was a household name.

Hänsel und Gretel is a masterpiece of music-theatre, fusing one of
the most opulent scores in German opera to one of the best known
fairy tales in Western culture. To complement the style of the tale

Humperdinck borrowed liberally from German folk songs, and the opera's more memorable melodies owe much to the simplicity of the slow-moving, four-bar, narrow-interval tunes of the German vernacular tradition. One tune, in particular, acts as a fulcrum for the whole score: the children's songs and dances, the idyllic forest scenes, the comically supernatural material involving the Witch and the central chorale are all forged from a single folk-based theme – indeed, some would say that its over-insistent repetition is the opera's chief weakness. It also has to be said that the dense Wagnerian texture can at times seem over-complicated for the subject matter, but there are many magical episodes in which Humperdinck demonstrates exceptional imagination and technique. The finest orchestral writing occurs in the almost cinematic orchestral interludes – the breathtaking "Witch's Ride" (Act I), the haunting "Dream Pantomime" (Act II), and the evocative prelude to the final act, during which the children are awakened by the Dew Fairy. Ultimately, however, *Hänsel und Gretel* is above all a showcase for the female voice, as the Father is the only male part, although the mezzo-soprano Witch is sometimes taken by a character tenor. The siblings themselves are captivatingly sugary soprano roles, to whom the majority of the opera's pivotal music is assigned. The Witch is great fun, and her low-lying music gives a suitably theatrical singer plentiful opportunity to hurl out her words in a semi-sung style.

Kurt Eichorn's performance for RCA is daringly unsentimental, and his cast is unbeatable. To have been able to engage Lucia Popp as the Dew Fairy and Arleen Augér as the Sandman – both small roles – suggests an embarrassment of riches. The only slight let-down is Anna Moffo's somewhat shrill Hänsel, but so wonderfully rich is Helen Donath's portrayal of Gretel, and so outrageous Christa Ludwig's pantomime Witch that Moffo's unsteady tone is a small dent in an otherwise flawless performance of the vocal score. Eichorn very sensibly pushes where most conductors relax, and he creates a genuinely theatrical atmosphere, memorably so during the interludes, which are here given womderfully colourful readings. The orchestra give an outstanding performance, and the recording reflects the conductor's amazing attention to instrumental and vocal balance.

37

Leoš Janáček

Jenůfa

Elisabeth Söderström (Jenůfa), Eva Randová (Kostelnička), Petr Dvorský (Števa), Wieslaw Ochman (Laca); Vienna State Opera Chorus; Vienna Philharmonic Orchestra; Charles Mackerras (conductor)

Decca 414 483-2; 2 CDs; full price

Jenůfa was Janáček's first opera to make it to the stage and, for half a century after his death, it was his only work to be performed with any frequency. It was inspired by the work of Gabriela Preissová, a pivotal figure in the history of Czech theatre, whose early "slice of life" dramas *The Farm Manager's Woman* and *Her Foster-Daughter* caused a stir during the 1890s. Janáček was beaten to the former by his rival Josef Foerster, but he successfully secured the rights to the latter in 1902, and began work on the score a year later. The resulting work was hailed as the blossoming of a truly Czech style of opera.

Preissová's tale is solemn stuff. Jenůfa is made pregnant by the drunken layabout Števa. Jenůfa's foster-mother, Kostelnička, announces that they can marry only after Števa has remained sober for a year. Jenůfa rejects the advances of the jealous Laca, who slashes her face with a knife. Kostelnička then places Jenůfa in hiding until the birth of her child – by which time Števa has become engaged to the mayor's daughter. Realizing that Laca loves Jenůfa, but that the baby stands in the way of their marriage, Kostelnička throws the child into the river, telling Jenůfa that it died soon after the birth. On her wedding day to Laca, a baby's body is found under the melting ice. Jenůfa is accused of murder, but Kostelnička steps forward and confesses her crime.

Jenůfa forgives her, and she and Laca resolve to face the world together.

In its dramatic power and hard-hitting subject matter, *Jenůfa* has affinities with the work of Puccini, whose operas were regularly performed in central Europe at that time – indeed the premiere of *Jenůfa* in Brno was followed the next night by a performance of *Tosca*. However, the musical styles of Puccini and Janáček are sharply contrasted, partly for linguistic reasons: Italian is full of long vowels which in music get translated into sustained melodic lines, while Czech is heavy with consonants and percussive rhythms which suggest short but powerful musical phrases. The musical representation of natural speech is a crucial aspect of this opera. "At the time *Jenůfa* was being composed," Janáček wrote, "I drank in the melodies of the spoken word. Furtively, I listened to the speech of passers-by, reading the expression of their faces, following with my eyes every raised voice, noticing the speakers' environment, their company, the time of day, whether it was light or dark, cold or warm. I also rejoiced quietly at the beauty of these speech melodies, at their aptness and the ampleness of their expression."

Thus Janáček's vocal lines are declamatory rather than conventionally melodic, and the orchestral score is no less severe, with slowly moving orchestral blocks providing a strong tonal background for the development of character and dialogue. If this all sounds rather heavy going then it is to be remembered that Janáček was more interested in moving his audiences than entertaining them – to which end *Jenůfa* is arguably his most powerful testament.

Mackerras's 1982 recording of *Jenůfa* brings the necessary emotional drive and rhythmic bite to the proceedings, and the Viennese orchestra and chorus respond with electrifying precision and energy. Sopranos Elisabeth Söderström and Eva Randová are splendid foils as Jenůfa and Kostelnička; likewise the tenors Petr Dvorský and Wieslaw Ochman create a striking impression as Števa and Laca. The score's most powerful scenes, such as Jenůfa's final address, are exceptionally vivid – thanks, not least, to the flawless recorded sound.

38

Leoš Janáček

The Cunning Little Vixen

Lucia Popp (Vixen), Eva Randová (Fox), Dalibor Jedlička (Gamekeeper);
Vienna State Opera Chorus; Vienna Philharmonic Orchestra; Charles
Mackerras (conductor)

Decca 417 129-2; 2 CDs; full price

Of Janáček's nine operas, the four greatest were composed during the decade preceding his death in 1928, at the age of 74. By far the sunniest and the most tuneful of these is *The Cunning Little Vixen*. Janáček had recently completed the angst-ridden *Kát'a Kabanová* when, in 1921, he turned by way of relief to *Bystrouška* (Sharp-Ears), a popular newspaper cartoon strip written by Rudolf Těsnohlídek. Unlike many anthropomorphic tales, these stories were not satirical in intent, but simply an evocation of country life in Moravian dialect. They were particularly appealing to Janáček, who in 1921 had bought a house in his native village of Hukvaldy, where walks in the surrounding countryside provided relaxation and inspiration. Once his attention had been drawn to the strip, Janáček started a special study of animals, noting down, no doubt, their "speech melodies". Janáček fashioned his own libretto and achieved a melding of the human and animal worlds that enabled them to interact without coyness, but he made a significant departure from his source, which ends with the vixen's courtship and wedding – Janáček kills the vixen in Act III, thereby expanding his subject into the cycle of birth, death and rebirth.

The tale is set in a forest, where a Gamekeeper, awakened by a frog, captures the Vixen and takes her home for his children.

The Vixen escapes back to the forest, where she evicts a badger so as to spy on the Gamekeeper and his friends. She meets the Fox; they fall in love and marry. The Gamekeeper sets a trap, which is mocked by the Vixen and her new family. While stealing chickens from the poultry farm, the Vixen is shot dead by the Gamekeeper. The Gamekeeper lies down to sleep on his way home and dreams of a young vixen. He tries to catch her, but succeeds only in grabbing hold of a frog. The frog says it was his grandfather last time round and he'd told him about the Gamekeeper.

In keeping with its rural theme, *The Cunning Little Vixen* relies heavily on folk-like melodies, but it is also one of the more experimental of Janáček's scores. The piece moves between opera, ballet, mime and orchestral interludes, with a number of recurring melodic patterns and motifs unifying the whole work. The predominant sound is of the luscious strings that evoke the forest, while idiosyncratic figures in the woodwind and solo violin characterize specific creatures. The vocal score is largely dictated by the rhythm and metre of Czech speech, which gives it its distinctive flavour, but Janáček also uses melody to characterize each of the animals: in particular, the Vixen's soprano role is notable for its great energy and beauty, and the way in which Janáček gives the impression of a scurrying animal without sacrificing beauty of line is magical. The whole effect is novel, fresh and life-affirming – the composer speaks through the Gamekeeper, who observes as he falls asleep that "men and women will walk with heads bowed, and realize that a more-than-earthly joy has passed that way."

Mackerras's 1981 recording is demonstration-quality Janáček. Lucia Popp, as the Vixen, is youthful and mercurial; Eva Randová is understated as the Fox and Dalibor Jedlička is refreshingly down-to-earth as the Gamekeeper. Particular highlights include Popp's rapture as the Vixen becomes aware of and revels in her beauty; the joyful wedding, complete with the wordless singing forest; and Jedlička's matter-of-fact final remarks. Luxuriant and permeated with a glowing warmth, this recording is probably the place for newcomers to Janáček to start.

39

Leoš Janáček

The Makropulos Case

Elisabeth Söderström (Emilia Marty), Petr Dvorský (Albert Gregor), Václav Zítek (Jaroslav Prus); Vienna Philharmonic Orchestra; Charles Mackerras (conductor)

Decca 430 372-2; 2 CDs; full price

The writer Karel Čapek was sceptical when Janáček approached him for the rights to *The Makropulos Case*: the legalistic paraphernalia at the centre of his play did not seem to lend itself to operatic treatment, and the modern-day setting of offices, theatres and hotel rooms seemed especially unconducive to a composer of Janáček's folkloric proclivities. "That old crank," he joked, "soon he'll be setting the local column in the newspaper." (Janáček had already done just that, of course, with *The Cunning Little Vixen*.) But when the playright saw the premiere in Brno he was obliged to admit: "He did it a hundred times better than I could ever have imagined." In complete contrast with the sprightliness and optimism of *The Cunning Little Vixen*, this opera is a poignant evocation of world-weariness.

The curtain rises on the office of the lawyer Dr Kolenatý, who is awaiting the outcome of the century-old inheritance case of Gregor versus Prus. Kolenatý outlines the case at length to the famous opera singer Emilia Marty, who reveals an uncanny knowledge of past events concerning Elian MacGregor, the mistress of "Pepi" Prus, and directs them to an unknown will. It turns out that Marty, having been forced to test an elixir of life by her alchemist father, has been alive, in various guises, for more than three hundred years. Fearful that the formula has begun to fade, she goes to great lengths to procure from Kolenatý the original formula, which forms part of the estate being contested by Gregor vs Prus. After giving herself to Prus, who is horrified by her coldness, she gains the formula but realizes that she has tired of life and wishes to die. As she dies she gives the formula to the young singer Kristina, who burns it.

The Makropulos Case opens with a wonderful prelude full of sweeping strings, brass and timpani, with offstage fanfares and drums harking back to the distant world of Rudolf II (Emilia was born in 1585, to the alchemist of Rudolf's court). Having deployed his full resources in this effusive, lyrical outburst, Janáček holds it all back, keeping the music dry and rather spare until the conclusion – there are no duets or ensembles, and there's a high level of dissonance, making this one of the composer's more arduous scores at first hearing. Janáček saves the most heartfelt music for the end, with Emilia's overwhelming confession and renunciation of her immortality. The brass and drums of the opening return with an incredible feeling of inevitability, and Janáček brings it all out of reserve as warm and cathartic string phrases surge beneath Emilia's cool resignation, making her seem for the first time human and vulnerable. Janáček is determined to warm up a heroine he described as "the icy one" – clearly reflecting the composer's ambivalent feelings about Kamila Stösslová, the young woman for whom he conceived an unreciprocated (but artistically fruitful) passion in the final decade of his life.

Emilia Marty should dominate the proceedings throughout, and that is exactly what Elisabeth Söderström does in this classic 1978 recording. The supporting male roles of lawyers, clerks and claimants are well sung by artists who are regulars on Mackerras's Janáček recordings: Petr Dvorský, Vladimir Krejčik, Václav Zítek and Dalibor Jedlička. Beno Blachut is excellent in the one comic role, Emilia's former lover Hauk-Šendorf. As usual Mackerras judges the pacing to perfection, and like all in this Decca series, the set has very full essays by John Tyrrell, the leading expert on Janáček; the early *Lachian Dances* are included as a fill-up.

40

Erich Korngold

Die tote Stadt

René Kollo (Paul), Carol Neblett (Marie/Marietta), Benjamin Luxon (Frank);
Bavarian Radio Chorus; Munich Radio Orchestra; Erich Leinsdorf (conductor)

RCA GD87767; 2 CDs; mid-price

Only a handful of Erich Wolfgang Korngold's works are performed with any regularity, yet between 1916 and 1933 he was Austria's most celebrated composer, and *Die tote Stadt* (The Dead City) was the city's most frequently performed modern opera. Korngold began setting a libretto by one Paul Schott, based on George Rodenbuch's symbolist novel *Bruges-la-morte*, in 1917, aged only 19. He completed it two years later, and in 1920 it was given simultaneous premieres in Cologne and Hamburg. The German public was amazed that such a young man was capable of writing music of such melancholy; many were incredulous when it emerged that Korngold was also the elusive Mr Schott.

The libretto is maudlin stuff. Paul is in mourning for his dead wife, Marie, rarely leaving his house and preserving a room as a shrine to her memory. His best friend Frank persuades him to take a walk into Bruges, during which he sees Marietta, a *Doppelgänger* of his wife. They meet and Paul begins to believe that his wife has returned to him. When she sees a portrait of Marie, Marietta begins to mock Paul for his stupidity. That night Paul has a vision in which Marie begs him to "see and understand". There follows a lengthy dream sequence which ends with Paul strangling Marietta with a length of her hair. When he wakes, the plait is in his hands but Marietta is nowhere to be seen. He understands Marie's riddle and, changing out of his black suit, he leaves the city.

As an examination of the pain of separation and the grieving process *Die tote Stadt* is an unforgettably intense experience, and remarkably profound for a man of such youth. Korngold's score is sometimes dismissed as being too sentimental, and the mixture of quasi-religious melancholy and chromatic sweetness can be a bit much for those with ascetic tastes. But the sincerity of - this opera is unmistakeable, and the precision with which Korngold marshals the huge orchestral forces is unforgettably striking, as is the inventiveness of the structure, with its brilliantly evocative series of leitmotifs. That said, *Die tote Stadt* is celebrated above all for the simple beauty of the vocal score. The opera's highlight, and one of the opera's cyclical motifs, is the Act I duet, "Gluck, das mir verblieb" (Joy, sent from above). This inspired episode – made famous in 1924 through a recording with Lotte Lehmann and Richard Tauber – illuminates Paul's despair, and his undying love for Marie, with heartbreaking clarity; when, at the opera's close, Paul bids farewell to Marie and their home, with a restatement of the duet's chorus, it is difficult not to give in to the swell of emotion. The opera is not all crushed velvet, however. Paul's dream sequence, for example, is portrayed through music of unsettling, dissonant starkness, and his murder of the imaginary Marie is a genuinely shocking episode amid the generally lush landscape of Korngold's music.

Erich Leinsdorf's 1975 recording of *Die tote Stadt* has never left the catalogue and, for many, it is his finest achievement. His tempi are ideal throughout, and he brings remarkable clarity to the huge washes of orchestral sound. He also provides excellent support for the leading couple, René Kollo (Paul) and Carol Neblett (Marietta), and perhaps for this reason, the performance reflects remarkably well on Kollo's tenor voice, which rarely sounds its best on record. Neblett is in glowing form, tapping the sentimentality with shameless abandon, Benjamin Luxon makes a wonderfully tender and meditative Frank, and the recording is excellent.

41

Franz Lehár

Die lustige Witwe

Cheryl Studer (Hanna Glawari), Boje Skovhus (Danilo), Bryn Terfel (Mirko Zeta), Barbara Bonney (Valencienne); Vienna Philharmonic Orchestra; John Eliot Gardiner (conductor)

Deutsche Grammophon 439 911-2; 1 CD; full price

In terms of his financial success, Franz Lehár was the Andrew Lloyd-Webber of his day. *Die lustige Witwe* (The Merry Widow) was a universally popular work, with admirers as diverse as Adolf Hitler and Albert Einstein, and it made its composer a dollar millionaire – and, at the same time, revitalized the flagging world of Viennese operetta. First performed in 1905, *Die lustige Witwe* is the quintessential operetta: it has a plot full of misunderstandings and tingling emotional encounters, an exotic setting, and more hit tunes than any other light opera outside the oeuvre of Johann Strauss the Younger (see p.151). Initially, however, the odds were against its success. The director of the Theater an der Wien was horrified by Lehár's risqué creation and offered the composer a large sum of money to withdraw it. When Lehár refused, the theatre gave it the cheapest possible production, with second-hand costumes and sets. The first night went well enough, but business was slow and it looked as if the work would be dropped; eventually, however, word got around, and within six months it was Vienna's most popular new work.

Its colossal success owed much to Victor Léon and Leo Stein's sexy libretto. The Pontevedrian widow Hanna Glawari, living in Paris, is left a fortune, but it is essential to her country's finances that she marries a Pontevedrian. Mirko Zeta, the Pontevedrian Ambassador in Paris – whose wife Valencienne is being pursued by Camille de Rosillon – orders his attaché Count Danilo to marry Hanna. They had been in love before, but he has vowed never to say "I love you". After much intrigue, the two are married and Pontevedro is saved.

Die lustige Witwe is celebrated for its easy and memorable tunes, and for its luxuriant local colour: the Pontevedrian characters are associated with east-European style mazurkas, polonaises and kolos; Paris is evoked through the galope and can can; while Viennese marches and waltzes occupy the middle ground. But Lehár's score is also strikingly innovative. Most operetta composers used little more than an augmented chamber orchestra, but *The Merry Widow* calls for harp, glockenspiel and tambourine in the pit, plus guitar, tambourine and strings on stage, in addition to a sumptuous orchestra of quadruple woodwind, brass and strings. Lehár also knew how to use these forces, and there are some remarkably inventive episodes. When, for example, Hanna and Danilo finally get together in Act III the solo violin and cello symbolically intertwine while the music slips into a seductive waltz that underpins their relationship throughout the piece.

John Eliot Gardiner made his reputation with Renaissance and Baroque music, but this fizzing recording of *The Merry Widow* indicates a very broad talent. The Vienna Philharmonic sound as if they have this music in their blood (though in fact they hadn't touched it for forty years prior to this performance) and Gardiner encourages the string section to indulge the swooping and sliding for which the city's performances of operetta used to be famous. His cast bring a quality of unforced clarity and ease to the vocal lines and show the wisdom of bringing opera singers into this repertoire – only Boje Skovhus has been a regular performer of operetta. The vocal highlights fall largely to the soprano voices of Barbara Bonney and Cheryl Studer, whose portrayal of Hanna is unforgettably touching. This recording's other great plus is that the score is uncut, and yet fits on a single CD. A lot of the spoken dialogue has been axed, but this is very much a blessing in disguise.

Ruggero Leoncavallo

I Pagliacci

Franco Corelli (Canio), Lucine Amara (Nedda), Tito Gobbi (Tonio), Mario
Zanasi (Silvio); Chorus and Orchestra of La Scala; Lovro von Matačić (conductor)

EMI CMS7 63967–2; 2 CDs, with *Cavalleria rusticana*; full price

Mascagni's *Cavalleria rusticana* (see
p.89) is credited with having
launched *verismo* opera in 1890,
but apotheosis of the genre came
two years later, when Leoncavallo's
I Pagliacci (The Clowns) was given
its first performance, conducted by
the young Arturo Toscanini, to an
ecstatic Milan audience. Such was
the applause, both during and after
the performance, that the seventy-minute piece lasted half the
night. Leoncavallo was not surprised: the fashion for short, true-
to-life operatic dramas was at its height, and he knew he had written a piece that was even more intense than Mascagni's rustic
soap-opera. But Leoncavallo's success had been a long time coming. His earliest operas – including *Crepusculum*, a Renaissance trilogy in the style of Wagner's *Ring* cycle – had all failed, and he had
toyed with the idea of becoming a librettist. His prose, however,
was even less popular than his music (Puccini dropped him as the
librettist for *Manon Lescaut*), and had it not been for the success of
Cavalleria rusticana Leoncavallo might have abandoned the stage
altogether.

In 1891 his magistrate father told him about a case concerning
infidelity and murder within a troupe of itinerant actors.
Leoncavallo cleverly manipulates the material by presenting
Pagliacci as a play within a play. The curtain rises on Tonio, who
informs us that we are about to witness a true story. As he

retreats into the shadows a crowd of villagers gathers to welcome the players and their director, Canio. It emerges that Canio's wife, Nedda, is having an affair with Silvio. Tonio overhears their banter and informs Canio of their plans to meet in private. When Canio confronts his wife she denies the accusation, and Canio pours out his heart to the audience. The second act begins with Canio and his troupe performing a drama for the villagers that mirrors their own situation. Reality and fantasy blend as the drama comes to an end with Canio murdering both his wife and Silvio on stage. "Bravo!" shout the villagers.

Leoncavallo's style is significant for the brevity of the musical lines and for the intensity of each character's expression. He forgoes the long, indulgent melodies exploited so successfully by Verdi and Puccini. This is not to say that *I Pagliacci* lacks tunes – nothing could be farther from the truth – but the music is constantly on a knife-edge, requiring the singers to hurl themselves into Leoncavallo's melodramatic writing. In particular, the clown Canio is one of the most exhilarating Italian tenor roles, requiring a singer with stamina, flexibility and power. He and the opera in general are celebrated for the brief lament "Vesti la giubba" (Put on the costume), an outburst of shivering self-pity, but his opening monologue and the concluding, feverishly passionate "No, pagliaccio, non son!" (No, I am not a clown) have even greater dramatic impact. The rest of the cast – the spitting, hissing, seductive Nedda, the creepy Tonio, the deeply unlovely Silvio – make sure that the action stays way over the top.

Made in 1960, this magnificent recording boasts a fabulous performance from Franco Corelli. His diction is almost comically lazy, but the thrill of his voice is like no other, and with the threatening "No, pagliaccio, non son!" he brings the drama to a uniquely fevered pitch. As Nedda, Lucine Amara does well to keep pace, and Tito Gobbi is outstanding as Tonio. The only drawback is the somewhat anonymous direction from Lovro von Matačić, but for the elemental theatricality of the singing there is nothing to rival this classic performance. The accompanying *Cavalleria rusticana*, however, is a great disappointment considering the assemblage of talent.

43

György Ligeti

Le Grand Macabre

Willard White (Nekrotzar), Sibylle Ehlert (Gepopo/Venus), Charlotte Hellekant (Amando), Laura Claycomb (Amanda), Jard van Nes (Mescalina), Derek Lee Ragin (Prince Go-Go); London Sinfonietta Voices; Philharmonia Orchestra; Esa-Pekka Salonen (conductor)

Sony S2K 62312; 2 CDs; full price

In 1965 the Stockholm Opera commissioned Ligeti to write an opera based on the story of Oedipus, but when Ligeti's librettist died he abandoned the project for a new subject – Michel de Ghelderode's *La balade du grand macabre*. Ghelderode's play appealed to Ligeti for its fantasy landscape and for having Death as the hero, but Ligeti was less enthusiastic about its poetic language and asked the producer Michel Meschke to "Jarry-fy" it, that is to give it the absurdity and viciousness of the work of Alfred Jarry. It's a spiky and surreal creation with a vein of social commentary running through it – *Le Grand Macabre* can be seen as a kind of critique of solipsistic 1960s hedonism, with its drug-named characters and its sexually over-active lovers. As Ligeti once wrote: "Life utterly devoid of fear, life entirely devoted to pleasure, is in fact profoundly sad."

Evoking the nightmare visions of Hieronymus Bosch and Pieter Breughel the Elder, the opera tells of the attempts of the tyrannical Nekrotzar (the "Grand Macabre") to destroy a world populated by such figures as the young Prince Go-Go of Breughelland, the libidinous Mescalina, and Amanda and Amando, a couple devoted to non-stop lovemaking (they were originally called Clitoria and Spermando). The astrologer Astradamor predicts that a comet will devastate the earth at midnight, but its arrival passes safely and

Nekrotzar allows Prince Go-Go to lead him back to the grave. Death doesn't triumph at the end, but there is little reassurance in the conclusion: "No-one knows when his hour will fall. And when it comes, then let it be . . . Farewell, till then, live merrily!"

Ligeti's score for *Le Grand Macabre* is suitably polymorphous. To emphasize the piece's irrationality, there is no consistent musical idiom; instead the music darts around all over the place, encompassing the shimmering orchestral textures which one associates with Ligeti's concert pieces, through moments of clamorous expressionism, by way of parodies of and quotations from other works. Ligeti was trying to get away from the grandiloquent gestures of traditional opera: "the dramatic action and the music should be riskily bizarre, totally exaggerated, totally crazy . . . The musical and dramatic conception should be far removed from the territory of Wagner, Strauss and Berg." To establish a mock-heroic mood, the opera opens with a palindromic fanfare of car horns, before Piet the Pot enters singing the "Dies irae". The most lyrical passages in the opera are in the music given to the two lovers (both sung by sopranos), which resembles the most sensuous moments of Monteverdi's *Poppea* carried to absurd extremes of ecstatic ornamentation. Nekrotzar's entrance in Act II is accompanied by an orchestral interlude based on the finale of Beethoven's *Eroica* symphony. Such use of allusion is incorporated into the fabric of the work in a way that Ligeti himself has compared to the use of "borrowed" material in Pop Art. Irony and knowingness are all, but *Le Grand Macabre* also possesses an exuberant energy and naiveté that makes it highly enjoyable.

In 1997 Ligeti fully revised his original score. He cut quite a bit of music and a large amount of spoken dialogue, wrote music for roles that had previously been spoken, and generally increased the melodic content. Sony's 1999 recording of this revised version features A-list operatic stars Willard White, Derek Lee Ragin and Jard van Nes, whose lyrical talents are well suited to the softer *Grand Macabre* – although each is required to do some less ingratiating work, ranging from mumbling to screaming. Salonen provides energetic direction, and the Philharmonia cope superbly with the score's many original demands.

44

Jean-Baptiste Lully

Armide

Guillemette Laurens (Armide), Howard Crook (Renaud), Bernard Deletré (Hidraot/Ubalde); La Chapelle Royale; Collegium Vocale; Philippe Herreweghe (conductor)

Harmonia Mundi HMC901456.57; 2 CDs; full price

Few men have dominated any artistic milieu to the extent that Lully dominated the French music scene during the reign of Louis XIV. Through his friendship with the king, and some unscrupulous wheeler-dealing, he managed to achieve almost complete control of the musical life of Paris and Versailles. Between 1672 and 1687 he was the sole composer of French opera, and thus was entirely responsible for forging a national operatic style: a style that was rooted in formal and grandiose court spectacle, yet at the same time was concerned to convey the text in as clear and direct a fashion as possible. Five acts long, Lully's operas were introduced by sycophantic prologues that highlighted recent events in the Sun King's life and invariably had nothing to do with the ensuing drama, which would present a well-known mythological or chivalric tale with plenty of supernatural elements, providing wonderful opportunities for elaborate scenic effects.

Armide (Armida) is generally reckoned to be Lully's greatest dramatic achievement. Philippe Quinault's libretto is based on episodes from Tasso's *Gerusalemme liberata*, a sixteenth-century chivalric verse epic that was extremely popular with composers at the time – indeed, the story of Rinaldo and Armida had been set several times before Lully's version. Set in Damascus during the First Crusade, it tells of how Hildraoth (Hidraot), King of Damascus, and the sorceress Armida (Armide) plan to kill Rinaldo (Renaud), general of the victorious crusaders. Armida, however, falls in love with Rinaldo, who is rescued from her enchanted palace by two of his fellow knights. Armida in despair summons demons to destroy her palace.

In common with Lully's earlier masterpiece *Atys*, *Armide* contains extraordinary "sommeil" scenes, in which the hero is lulled into a deep sleep as a prelude to being bewitched, and both contain a female protagonist with supernatural powers who is rejected by the object of her desire, thus precipitating her fury. But the character of Armida is a more rounded one than Cybele, with far greater psychological depth. The role was first performed by Marie Le Rochois, one of Lully's regular singers, who created a sensation with her very first entry, and whose final desperate solo – a tour de force of emotional abandon – produced a profound effect on its first audience. The Lully-Quinault style of recitative – a style more melodious and fluid than the Italian model from which it was derived – reaches its peak in this opera, and the internal conflict expressed by Armida as she attempts to kill the sleeping Rinaldo was regarded by eighteenth-century writers, including Rameau, as the absolute model of the form. The opera's ending was unique among Lully's works in that, although it contained a spectacular *coup de thèâtre* in the destruction of Armida's palace, its closing moments were intimate and tragic – despite the fact that the hero Rinaldo has escaped the sorceress's clutches.

No recording of a Lully opera can represent anything like the totality of the proceedings, but Herreweghe's elegant and persuasive performance goes a long way to making Lully's music seem dramatically feasible on its own. There is a great deal of contrast and variety here, ranging from the sprightly rhythms of the ever-present dance music to the meltingly beautiful prelude at the beginning of the third scene of Act II. Herreweghe, whose reputation is as a choral conductor, is well served by his soloists, with the forceful Guillemette Laurens brilliant at conveying the ambivalent emotions of Armida, nowhere more powerfully than in her final scene, which wavers between rage and despair. Howard Crook's Rinaldo is necessarily rather bloodless, but he has an unerringly elegant sense of the music's line.

45

Pietro Mascagni

Cavalleria rusticana

José Carreras (Turiddù), Montserrat Caballé (Santuzza), Matteo Manuguerra (Alfio), Astrid Varnay (Mamma Lucia); Ambrosian Opera Chorus; Philharmonia Orchestra; Riccardo Muti (conductor)

EMI CMS7 63650-2; 2 CDs; with *I Pagliacci*; mid-price

During the 1880s there emerged a new strain of Italian opera known as *verismo*, in which grittily realistic characters were depicted in situations of extreme stress, to the accompaniment of brief, illustrative outbursts of music. Of the various elements that fed this brief-burning flame one of the most significant was the literary realism of writers such as Dumas, Zola and the Sicilian author Giovanni Verga. Italian composers were particularly taken by Verga's brutal tales and in 1889 Pietro Mascagni decided to turn Verga's novella *Cavalleria rusticana* (Rustic Chivalry) into a one-act opera. The completed work lasted no more than seventy minutes, but its impact on audiences, and the course of Italian opera, was immense. Yet had Mascagni's wife not played a hand, *Cavalleria rusticana* might never have been heard of. Mascagni wrote the opera at speed in 1889 in response to an advertisement for a one-act opera competition being promoted by the publisher Sonzogno. Seized by doubts as to the opera's quality he determined to send in the fourth act of an earlier, inferior opera called *Guglielmo Ratcliffe*. Without his knowledge Mascagni's wife submitted *Cavalleria rusticana* instead, and the rest is history. Like every other *verismo* composer Mascagni never again tasted comparable success, but as he once conceded it was "better to have conquered once, than never to have conquered at all."

Set in a Sicilian village on Easter morning, *Cavalleria* has the prototypical *verismo* plot. Turiddù has returned from the army to discover that his lover, Lola, has married Alfio. He has found consolation with Santuzza, who has borne him a child. Turiddù still loves Lola, however, and rejects Santuzza's declaration of love. Seeking revenge, she tells Alfio that Lola has been unfaithful with Turiddù. Alfio challenges Turiddù to a duel. After bidding farewell to his mother, whom he asks to care for Santuzza, Turiddù fights Alfio and is killed.

In outline *Cavalleria rusticana* has obvious similarities with that other definitve *verismo* opera, Leoncavallo's *I Pagliacci*, with which it is often paired in a double-bill known to opera buffs as *Cav and Pag*. Yet Mascagni's opera is a more civilized experience, with little of the drama's violence manifested in the score. Indeed, if *I Pagliacci* is the finer work of theatre, then *Cavalleria rusticana* is the finer piece of music. The wistful and often-excerpted Intermezzo is the most celebrated example of Mascagni's flair for an ingratiating tune, but even at the peak of tension, such as Turiddù's farewell to his mother, Mascagni spins long arches of pensive melody, whereas Leoncavallo favours an almost exclamatory intensity. The lengthy duet between Turiddù and Santuzza is typical in its repetition and development of a single, unbroken tune, and the prevailing lyricism is so seductive that you're drawn to the characters no matter how stupid or venal their behaviour.

Like most other *verismo* operas *Cavalleria rusticana* makes punishing demands of its cast, but it is also an opera that requires a strong conductor to keep the pace rapid. There has been none stronger than Riccardo Muti, who pushes the drama with great intensity, memorably so during his laudably unsentimental reading of the duet between Turiddù and Santuzza, a set-piece that flags in many other recordings. Carreras is a virile anti-hero and Montserrat Caballé is in beautiful voice as Santuzza. The same could not be said of Matteo Manuguerra's Alfio, but he is a marvellous vocal actor, bringing much-needed gravity to the role. The accompanying performance of *Pagliacci* (see p.83) is no less outstanding, running a close second to our first-choice recording.

46

Jules Massenet

Manon

Ileana Cotrubas (Manon), Alfredo Kraus (des Grieux), Gino Quilico (Lescaut); Chorus and Orchestra of the Capitole de Toulouse; Michel Plasson (conductor)

EMI CDS7 49610-2; 3 CDs; full price

Jules Massenet was one of the few French composers working during the last phase of the nineteenth century to remain true to the lineage of French lyric opera. Building on the work of Charles Gounod (see p.65), he brought a greater seriousness to his music and tightened the suave, self-consciously elegant vocal lines that were the hallmark of the French lyric style. The majority of his operas might have fallen into oblivion outside France, but his contribution to European opera represented one of the last great flowerings of Romantic music.

Saturated with what Ravel called the "pseudo-religious eroticism" of Gounod, Massenet's earliest works were the height of fashion, especially the exotic *Hérodiade*, a version of the Salome legend (as retold by Flaubert) in which the semi-declamatory melodies anticipate something of the vocal manner of Debussy's *Pelléas et Mélisande*, which would appear some twenty years later. For his next opera, *Manon*, he again turned to a celebrated piece of fiction (this time by Abbé Prévost), but there was little that was modern or exotic in his score. Rather, Massenet refined Gounod's style to a point of unprecedented theatricality, whereby the vocal lines were incorporated into an uninterrupted narrative, with fewer pauses for arias and a much darker, more intense vein of expression. It was an approach perfectly suited to

Prévost's portrayal of the seduction, imprisonment, ruin and death of Manon, of the disintegration, religious conversion and eventual fall of her lover des Grieux, and of the moral and emotional turmoil suffered by Manon's cousin, Lescaut.

Manon was vindication of Massenet's credo "the public is always right": in 1919, only seven years after the composer's death, it received its one-thousandth performance in France. Its popularity is chiefly attributable to the strikingly beautiful vocal score. Like Richard Strauss, Massenet was at his best writing for the female voice, and the title role is perhaps the fullest illustration of his facility for developing character: just compare her fragile first aria, an ingenuous passage revealing Manon's innocent enthusiasm for new experiences, with her Act III seduction aria, an urgent episode imbued with a sensuality that's far removed from the child-like creature of Act I. Des Grieux's tenor is not quite a match for the object of his devotion, even though his music is often potent enough, but Lescaut is that rare thing – a great French baritone role. The turmoil of the protagonists is set against a generally light orchestral backdrop, by which Massenet – making clever use of Baroque forms such as gavottes and minuets – conjures with remarkable clarity atmospheres as different as the devotional air of St-Sulpice and the sleaziness of the gaming rooms. For all the colour of its scene-painting, however, it is the emotional directness of the singing that makes *Manon* such a captivating opera.

The finest stereo recording of *Manon* is undoubtedly Michel Plasson's set with Ileana Cotrubas and Alfredo Kraus as the lovers. Neither lead singer is French, but they are both blessed with a real feeling for French style, and the long vocal lines are delivered with an ideal balance of sensuality and conviction. Gino Quilico's Lescaut is a believably noble creature, and the supporting cast are uniformly excellent. The Capitole de Toulouse Orchestra make the best of Massenet's rich writing for wind instruments, and Plasson underlines the great fluency of the score and keeps the cast and orchestra functioning as a single unit. The recording is wonderfully fresh but the full price is something of a shock considering this set was first released in 1982.

47

Jules Massenet

Werther

Alfredo Kraus (Werther), Tatiana Troyanos (Charlotte), Matteo Manguerra (Albert); London Philharmonic Orchestra; Michel Plasson (conductor)

EMI CMS7 69573-2; 2 CDs; mid-price

The protagonist of Goethe's *The Sorrows of Young Werther* is the archetypal Romantic hero, searching for truth and beauty while pining for an unattainable woman. The protagonist of the opera that Massenet made out of the novel is not much more than a victim of thwarted love, but if the more complex *Manon* is Massenet's greatest work of opera, *Werther* is his greatest work of music. He completed the score in 1887 but its production was delayed, firstly by the Opéra-Comique's management, who thought the work too depressing, and then by a gas-lamp which burnt down the theatre. *Werther* was eventually given its premiere in Vienna, where its musical quality was sufficient to overcome any misgivings about what a French composer might do to a German cultural masterwork.

Typically for the time, Massenet's libretto was a committee affair, with three acknowledged writers and a host of unnamed contributions, but for all the deviations from Goethe's text the basic structure remains the same. Shortly before leaving Frankfurt for an ambassadorial post the young poet Werther is introduced to Charlotte, the daughter of a widowed magistrate. He falls in love, little knowing that her fiancé Albert has only recently returned to the city. Charlotte cannot reciprocate Werther's love, much as she might like to, since she promised her dying mother that she would marry Albert. Werther spends the rest of the opera bemoaning his situation, and ends up shooting himself in despair. As he dies Charlotte confesses her love, and they kiss for the first and last time.

Three of the four acts occur around Christmas time, which enabled Massenet to make use of the sound of joyful children playing in the snow – to a point just short of the ridiculous at the opera's end, when the dying Werther mistakes them for angels. These episodes of somewhat cloying sentimentality are offset by the intense drama of Werther's urgent, unstable tenor. Although Werther's music is never anything other than tuneful – famously so in the aria "Pourquoi me réveiller?" (Why have you woken me?) at the end of Act III – his role is characterized above all by wide intervals and impassioned climaxes that provide the opera's most dramatic episodes. By contrast, Charlotte's struggle to resolve the conflicting claims of love and loyalty is bathed in music of intense, if occasionally sickly, sweetness. That said, Massenet's portrayal of her development from an inhibited and shy young girl to the woman who eventually declares her love to Werther (a moment that breaks with Goethe's novel, but which comes as a relief musically and dramatically) is quite moving. *Werther's* orchestrations are richer and weightier than in *Manon*, but they are never overbearing: rather the instrumental writing carries the vocal line with perfect fluency, creating a cohesiveness that is further underlined by Massenet's inventive use of motifs. All loose threads are audibly resolved during the final scenes in which, to music of throat-catching pathos, Werther is raised to heaven.

Michel Plasson's recording uses a London band, but he gets them to adopt French tone and phrasing, allowing the heavy orchestrations their due without letting them overwhelm things. His stylistic inclinations are well served by the mellifluous Alfredo Kraus (although the Spanish tenor's pronunciation is frequently wide of the mark), and he and Tatiana Troyanos make a perfect couple, with the latter's naturally rapid vibrato and dark tone nicely placed against Kraus's lighter voice. Manuguerra does well to hold back his formidable baritone as Albert, and he conveys just the right level of arrogance and cruelty. The sound is excellent and the price fair.

48

Claudio Monteverdi

Orfeo

John Mark Ainsley (Orpheus), Julia Gooding (Euridice), Catherine Bott (Music/Messenger/Proserpina); New London Consort; Philip Pickett (conductor)

L'Oiseau Lyre 433 545-2; 2 CDs; full price

If any person can be described as the founder of opera, it is Claudio Monteverdi. His work represents the culmination of an age of experiment, during which various Florentine scholars and musicians sought to recreate the dramatic traditions of the ancient world. The music-dramas that developed from these researches were high-minded but monotonous, whereas Monteverdi's operas offered a dramatic experience in which musical resources were fully deployed in the service of a theatrical text. Only three of his nineteen stage works have survived, but their power and imagination make them the only early operas to have firmly established a place in the modern repertory.

The most frequently revived of Monteverdi's works is *L'Orfeo, Favola in Musica* (Orpheus, a Fable in Music), which was almost certainly first performed in the Palazzo Ducale in Mantua, on February 24, 1607. The myth of Orpheus and Eurydice has always been a favourite for operatic treatment: its simple narrative and strong emotions are perfect for a genre that deals in extremes, and, of course, the protagonist embodies the transformational power of music. Furthermore, in Renaissance neo-Platonist philosophy the figure of Orpheus – who undergoes a kind of resurrection – was also identified with Christ, thus giving the tale an extra allegorical dimension. This opera may function on an esoteric level, but its greatest strength is the directness and the humanity of its drama. Monteverdi and his librettist remained true to the myth, in which the demi-god musician Orpheus descends to Hades to rescue his wife Eurydice, only to cause her death by turning to look at her on the journey back – although, perhaps to satisfy courtly taste, they created a happy ending.

In *Orfeo* Monteverdi follows Florentine precedent in making music the servant of the text. What makes him different from his forebears is the sheer inventiveness with which he pursues this end. Recitative is the dominant form of vocalizing, but it takes on many different guises, its flexibility deriving from the fact that the accompaniment is always subservient to the voice. The aria, as a clearly distinct vocal style, is not apparent in *Orfeo* as it is in Monteverdi's later operas; even the pivotal moment of the opera, "Possente spirto" (Powerful spirit), when Orpheus employs all his musical skill in order to enter Hades, is hardly melodic in a modern sense. Rather, what you hear is wonderfully ornamented declamation. The strongest melodies in *Orfeo* are found in the ritornelli, the short instrumental passages that punctuate the drama. Their name indicates the fact that they return, and, indeed, the opening ritornello, which re-occurs at the end of Act II and at the beginning of Act V, takes on an almost emblematic function, signifying both the world of mortals and the healing power of music. This symbolic aspect is also in evidence through the scoring, throughout which there is a clear distinction between the underworld, represented by darkly sonorous trombones, and the world of the living, which is scored mainly for strings.

From the sparkling attack of the opening "Toccata" it is clear that this is going to be a highly spirited performance. Pickett's conducting and the playing of his New London Consort are outstanding, successfully communicating both the intimacy of the drama and its idyllic freshness. Orpheus himself is a complex and self-absorbed character, qualities that are convincingly conveyed by John Mark Ainsley's finely judged performance, which communicates a real sense of Orpheus's power as a musician. Julia Gooding's delicate Euridice makes an ideal foil to Ainsley's more dynamic singing, and Catherine Bott subtly distinguishes her multiple roles of Music, the Messenger and Proserpina.

49

Claudio Monteverdi

Il Ritorno d'Ulisse in Patria

Christoph Prégardien (Ulisse), Bernarda Fink (Penelope), Christina
Högman (Telmaco), Lorraine Hunt (Minerva); Concerto Vocale; René
Jacobs (conductor)

Harmonia Mundi HMC 901 427.29; 3 CDs; full price

Il Ritorno d'Ulisse in Patria (The
Return of Ulysses to his
Homeland), the first opera to be
written by Monteverdi specifically
for the public opera houses of
Venice, opened at the Teatro Santi
Giovanni e Paolo early in 1640.
This work looks back to the classical world and courtly elegance
of *Orfeo* (see p.95), and yet it
inhabits a far more rugged landscape than its pastoral predecessor,
one peopled by more complex characters. With *Il Ritorno
d'Ulisse* Monteverdi rose magnificently to the challenge of writing for a relatively uninitiated audience: the convoluted plot,
with its vivid episodes and use of disguise, make the opera an
unprecedentedly theatrical event, and – more importantly – the
allegorical elements of his earlier work have given way to palpa-
bly human relationships.

The tale is based on the last ten books of Homer's *Odyssey*.
Ulysses's faithful wife Penelope, surrounded by suitors, laments
her husband's continued absence at the Trojan war. Ulysses arrives
in Ithaca and Minerva urges him to return to his home, which he
does disguised as a beggar. Penelope announces that she will
marry whoever successfully strings her husband's bow. The disguised Ulysses manages the feat, then proceeds to kill the suitors.

Like Orpheus, Ulysses is a hero who strives to be reunited
with his wife, but he is a warrior not an artist, and his struggles

are more physical than metaphysical. But by opening the opera with the trauma of Penelope's twenty-year abandonment, Monteverdi's librettist provides an ambivalent view of Ulysses's heroics. He also supplies the opera with elements that were already popular with Venetian audiences, like the special scenic effects of the Phaeacians' ship turning to stone, and the comic incidental characters, like the glutton Irus.

Monteverdi's musical response to this text was to an extent governed by his change of circumstances. He no longer had the splendid facilities of Mantua to call on, but instead had to work with a small pit orchestra that typically comprised about five strings, two theorbos (large lutes) and two harpsichords. (The two surviving manuscripts are both incomplete and neither of them indicates specific scoring, tempi or dynamics, and so these decisions are largely at the discretion of the conductor.) The instrumental ritornelli that were such an integral part of *Orfeo* have all but gone, and the choruses are greatly reduced. Instead there is much more emphasis on the exposed voice, either solo or in duets and trios: the final love duet between Penelope and Ulysses, with which the opera ends, was the prototype for what became a standard item of Venetian opera. Recitative still dominates and is used in several of the opera's most powerful moments, like Penelope's Act I monologue or her presentation of Ulysses's bow to the suitors in Act III. Arias are much more clearly defined than before and although Penelope has just one, at the end of Act III, it is the emotional highpoint of the opera, possessing a poignancy unmatched by anything in *Orfeo*.

As with most of Jacobs' opera recordings, this one derives from a stage production, and a lot of his musical decisions are a result of theatrical expedients. His is a very much darker and fuller sound-world than that created on the only rival set (conducted by Harnoncourt), and his singers are correspondingly more expressive. Bernarda Fink's Penelope borders on the neurotic, but the commitment of her performance pays off in the sheer cumulative intensity of the final scene, when Ulysses (a sweet-toned Prégardien) tries to convince her of his identity and she is torn between the desire to believe and her sense of honour.

50

Claudio Monteverdi

L'Incoronazione di Poppea

Sylvia McNair (Poppea), Diana Hanchard (Nerone), Anne Sofie von Otter (Ottavia), Michael Chance (Ottone); English Baroque Soloists; John Eliot Gardiner (conductor)

Archiv 447 088-2AH3; 3 CDs; full price

Monteverdi's last opera is the first opera to be located in the realm of history rather than that of mythology (although divine intervention continues to take place), and it inhabits a comprehensively different world from that of *Orfeo* or *Ulisse*. The world of *L'Incoronazione di Poppea* (The Coronation of Poppea) is one of sensuality and depravity, in which power is exercised without responsibility and lust triumphs over reason. This is also the most complex of Monteverdi's operas, with a cast of more than twenty characters, all of whom are affected by Poppea's unrelenting ambition and Nero's infatuation with her. Busenello's outstanding libretto is primarily derived from the historian Tacitus, whose writings, it has been suggested, provided the Venetian intelligentsia with a model for the presentation of the reality behind the masks of the great and beautiful. Many among the original audience would have been aware that the pregnant Poppea was kicked to death by Nero, a fact that makes the lovely closing duet grimly ironic.

The action is set in 62AD. Otho (Ottone) returns to Rome and his mistress Poppea, only to discover that she has been appropriated by Nerone. The philosopher Seneca sympathizes with the Emperor's wife, Octavia (Ottavia), and when he advises Nero not to divorce Octavia he is ordered to commit suicide.

The rejected Otho now turns his attentions to Drusilla, Poppea's lady-in-waiting. He is then ordered by Octavia to murder Poppea in her sleep. He disguises himself as Drusilla, in which guise he is spotted before he can carry out the deed. Drusilla is charged with the attempted crime and condemned to death. Otho is moved to confess, and he and Drusilla are exiled. Nero banishes Octavia and Poppea is crowned Empress.

The music for *Poppea* is more lyrical and contains more arias than Monteverdi's previous operas, but the narrative is still carried along by recitative. One of the great moments of the work is Octavia's first appearance when she sings the lament "Disprezzata regina" (Hated queen), a recitative pushed to the limits of expressiveness, in which changes of mood are indicated by changes of speed, and the use of rests between repeated phrases adds to the dramatic naturalism. Unsurprisingly the most sensuous lyricism occurs in the scenes between Nero and Poppea, with their final love duet justly celebrated as one of the supreme moments of seventeenth-century opera. Unfortunately the music of this duet is almost certainly not by Monteverdi nor the words by Busenello: Benedetto Ferrari, a contemporary of Cavalli, is usually credited with both, while other sections of the opera, the opening sinfonia for example, have been attributed to Cavalli himself. This is a measure of the freedom with which impresarios treated operas at that time, but it doesn't alter the fact that *Poppea* is the greatest achievement of Venetian opera, and the nearest it gets to the early ideal of a play enhanced by music. From here on music starts to assert itself as the dominant partner in opera's collaborative equation – increasingly to the detriment of clear meaning, if not of emotional impact.

Recorded live in 1993, the John Eliot Gardiner *Poppea* is unsurpassed for its immediacy and vitality. Gardiner conducts an orchestra that's smaller than the ensemble used on rival sets, which pushes the voices into particularly sharp relief. Sylvia McNair is a very sexy Poppea and Diana Hanchard makes an imperiously hard Nero, but Octavia and Otho tend to steal the show, as is so often the case. The always excellent Anne Sofie von Otter is especially moving in her long farewell to the city and her friends.

51

Wolfgang Amadeus Mozart

Die Entführung aus dem Serail

Arleen Augér (Constanze), Peter Schreier (Belmonte), Kurt Moll (Osmin);
Reri Grist (Blonde); Leipzig Radio Chorus; Dresden Staatskapelle; Karl
Böhm (conductor)

Deutsche Grammophon 429 868-2; 2 CDs; full price

The earliest of Mozart's operas to
have remained in the core repertoire is *Die Entführung aus dem
Serail* (The Escape from the
Harem), which was begun soon
after the 25-year-old composer
moved to Vienna in 1781. The
emperor Joseph II, who had suc-
ceeded Maria Theresa twelve
months earlier, had established a
German opera company in the city to rival the Italians who were
monopolizing the city's music scene. In 1781 Mozart was commissioned by this new company to write a *Singspiel* (a German
comic opera with spoken dialogue rather than recitative) on a
Turkish theme, there being a vogue for all things Ottoman at
that time. The director of the new theatre, Gottlieb Stephanie,
wrote the libretto himself and guided Mozart towards writing an
imitation of Turkish music as it was misunderstood at the time.
This curious phenomenon, known as "janissary music", involved
little more than the use of martial rhythms and quasi-oriental
percussion instruments, including a bell-covered stick known
throughout Europe as the "Jingling Johnny".

The mysterious East provided a richly spiced backdrop for
Stephanie's rescue scenario, in which Belmonte saves his long-lost
love Constanze (the name of Mozart's wife) and her servant
Blonde from the Pasha, his steward Osmin and the harem.
However, the style of *Die Entführung* is charming rather than con-

sistently "Oriental". Hero and heroine have big Italianate arias to sing, the servants are given folk songs, Pedrillo (Belmonte's servant) has a ballad in Act III that was added as something of a last-minute gesture, and the Pasha is a purely spoken role. The rhythm of the piece is also not as smooth as that of most of Mozart's later masterpieces: true to the conventions of *Singspiel*, the action is principally related through spoken dialogue, to which the arias and duets serve as commentary. For all that, each of the cast (except the Pasha) gets to sing exquisite and typically Mozartian melodies, even if, due to the less flexible construction of German poetry, the phrases are shorter and less ornate than those Mozart would later apply to Da Ponte's texts. Similarly beguiling is the atmosphere that Mozart imparts to the proceedings through the use of jangling janissary music and strange quasi-Middle Eastern modulations, while the punchy rhythms of the overture, ceremonial episodes and grand choruses add an extra dash of excitement.

Cohesion is brought to the proceedings by the character of the villainous Osmin who, though two arias, a song, a duet and a hand in the opera's four most important ensembles, enjoys a greater share of stage time than any of his colleagues. Belmonte, Blonde and Constanze might be rather conventional creations, adhering to the stock formulas of the time, but Constanze's coloratura soprano soars above the opera like the dove to which she is compared by Belmonte, and her eight-minute bravura aria "Martern aller Arten" (Tortures of every kind), with its dazzling accompaniment, is probably Mozart's greatest virtuoso vocal showpiece outside *Die Zauberflöte*.

Of the plentiful recordings currently available the finest is Karl Böhm's 1973 Dresden production. His treatment of the score's punchy rhythm and percussive orchestration is judged to perfection, and the Dresden orchestra provide a thrillingly dramatic backdrop – not least during Arleen Augér's blistering performance of "Martern aller Arten". Peter Schreier copes manfully with the almost feminine range of Belmonte's tenor and Kurt Moll is gloriously over the top as Osmin. The sense of connection between conductor, soloists and orchestra make this an example of ensemble opera at its very finest.

52

Wolfgang Amadeus Mozart

Le Nozze di Figaro

Cesare Siepi (Figaro), Hilde Gueden (Susanna), Alfred Poell (Count Almaviva), Lisa della Casa (Countess), Susanne Danco (Cherubino); Vienna State Opera Chorus; Vienna Philharmonic Orchestra; Erich Kleiber (conductor)

Decca 417 315-2DM3; 3 CDs; mid-price

Mozart's flirtation with German-style opera in *Die Entführung aus dem Serail* was short-lived. By the time he began to consider his next operatic project, Italian opera was again in vogue in Vienna, and he had been introduced to Lorenzo Da Ponte, the most gifted of the city's many resident Italian librettists. Da Ponte suggested an adaptation of Pierre Beaumarchais' sexually frank, politically subversive and recently banned play *La folle journée, ou Le mariage de Figaro*, having reassured the emperor that "anything that might offend good taste or public decency" would be removed from his libretto. In the event, Da Ponte retained the sexual intrigue but toned down the political angle – thus, for example, an outburst from Figaro about social injustice became a rant against the fickleness of women. He and Mozart also axed a few minor characters and scenes, but they added a dimension that had been missing in the original, a process summarized by Stendhal when he wrote that *Figaro* "transformed into real passions the superficial inclinations which amuse the easy-going inhabitants" of the Beaumarchais play.

The plot is a jumble of coincidences and mistaken identities set in eighteenth-century Spain. Count Almaviva's valet, Figaro, is to be married to the Countess's maid Susanna – who is being hotly pursued by the libidinous Count. The Count does everything he can to thwart their marriage (while the love-sick page boy Cherubino spends much of the opera chasing his wife) but the Count's schemes are forever outwitted by his wife and her trusty servants. The chaos leads to a fragile happy ending, in which the Count begs his wife's forgiveness, and the young lovers are able to wed.

The basic ingredients of *Figaro* are inherited from Italian comic opera, but Da Ponte's tailor-made text enabled Mozart to create a work that is far more subtle than these precursors, in which the divisions that traditionally separated arias, ensembles and recitative are broken down. This opera is a seamless unity – at every turn some change in tempo, key or setting resolves one episode while preparing the way for a new one. Above all, however, what makes this opera irresistible is that Mozart's protagonists possess real substance, thanks to his uncanny ability to devise melodies and orchestral accompaniments that lift even the plainest verbal utterance into the realm of poetic complexity. Listen to the Countess's aria at the start of Act II "Porgi amor, qualche ristoro" (God of love, grant me some remedy): the words do little more than establish the Countess's misery, but Mozart's music conjures such depths of yearning and desolation that in the space of a couple of minutes the opera acquires a wholly new emotional dimension. Act I could have been taken as a well-crafted knockabout, but from this point onwards there is the shadow of tragedy behind the farce. Such eloquence and economy of gesture is typical of an opera that remains, two centuries after its first performance, the most frequently performed of all operas.

There are dozens of recordings of *Figaro*, with many a curate's egg among them, but the finest ensemble production is Erich Kleiber's beautifully recorded and superbly played 1955 set for Decca. Kleiber was a theatrical conductor, and he brings infectious pace and energy to Mozart's score, while paying precise attention to the individual qualities of his cast – the like of which has not been seen since. In particular, Siepi and Gueden are matchless as Figaro and Susanna, with bags of personality to match the warmth of their voices, while Lisa della Casa is simply divine as the Countess. A sublime recording of a sublime opera.

53

Wolfgang Amadeus Mozart

Don Giovanni

Eberhard Waechter (Don Giovanni), Giuseppe Taddei (Leporello), Joan
Sutherland (Donna Anna), Elizabeth Schwarzkopf (Donna Elvira), Graziella
Sciutti (Zerlina), Luigi Alva (Ottavio); Philharmonia Chorus and Orchestra;
Carlo Maria Giulini (conductor)

EMI CDS7 47260-8; 3 CDs; full price

For their second collaboration
Mozart and Da Ponte settled on
the legend of the Stone Guest or,
as it is more commonly known,
Don Juan. Da Ponte might have
turned to any number of sources,
including plays by Tirso de
Molina, Molière and Goldoni, but
instead he levelled his sights on a
second-rate libretto by the third-
rate Giovanni Bertati, which was set to music in 1787 by one
Giuseppe Gazzanigna. He then consulted the world's greatest
seducer, Casanova, and successfully turned Bertati's sow's ear into
a silk purse. Mozart attached the subtitle *"dramma giocoso"* to *Don
Giovanni*, and viewed from a certain angle it is a comic tale of a
bad master and his bumbling attendant crashing from crisis to crisis. But the comedy in *Don Giovanni* is but a contrasting episode
to make the licentiousness and cruelty of the Don's career appear
yet darker. It's hardly surprising that, after its premiere in Vienna,
the emperor remarked to Mozart – "It is too difficult for the
singers and too tough for the teeth of the Viennese."

   The opera is set in motion by the Don's attempted rape of
Donna Anna and the murder of the Commendatore, her father.
Donna Anna and her fiancé Don Ottavio swear revenge on
Giovanni, but they are beaten to it by the Commendatore,
whose statue comes to life and drags the unrepentant libertine to

Hell. He more than earns this fate during the course of the opera for his treatment of the peasant girl Zerlina, Donna Elvira and his cowardly servant, Leporello.

Mozart wrote of *Don Giovanni*, "Whenever I sit at the piano with my new opera, I have to stop, for it stirs my emotions too deeply." It is indeed a relentlessly immediate work: every scene boasts at least one powerful aria or ensemble, and each character is vividly delineated by his or her own musical style, from the vengeful Donna Anna to the doting Ottavio. Beneath this multi-dimensional melody lies a tightly screwed orchestral score, a score characterized by an unusually percussive timbre and frequent aggressive instrumental interjections – all underlining the urgency of the drama and its deadly seriousness. And underlying every moment of the opera is the Manichean clash of the Don and the Commendatore: from the dread-filled opening of the overture the action is moving implacably towards their final confrontation, a course charted through the recurrence of the chords and tonalities with which they are associated.

The dominant figure is of course the Don himself, even though he has just two brief solos in the course of the entire opera: the seductive beauty of his serenade to Elvira's maid and the superhuman energy of his "champagne aria". Though chillingly adept at playing on the weaknesses of his prey, whether she be a coquettish country girl like Zerlina or a wary aristocrat like Donna Elvira, the Don explodes into animalistic violence when thwarted. Yet for all his barbarity the balance of sympathy is never tipped conclusively against the Don, and in his final moments he achieves something of the dark nobility of the fallen Lucifer.

Don Giovanni is Mozart's most melodramatic opera and Giulini's is the most melodramatic recording, full of exaggerated colour and generally fast-paced. Waechter's Don is the nastiest on record – he employs his huge voice with stinging, compulsive clarity. Taddei's multi-faceted Leporello can appear both repulsive and lovable within the space of ten bars, while the women – especially Sutherland's Donna Anna and Sciutti's Zerlina – are magnificent. This kaleidoscopic and viscerally exciting vision of *Don Giovanni* is an obvious first choice.

54

Wolfgang Amadeus Mozart

Così fan tutte

Véronique Gens (Fiordiligi), Bernarda Fink (Dorabella), Werner Güra (Ferrando), Marcel Boone (Guglielmo), Pietro Spagnoli (Don Alfonso), Graciela Oddone (Despina); Kölner Kammerchor; Concerto Köln; René Jacobs (conductor)

Harmonia Mundi HMC 951663.65; 3 CDs (plus free CD Rom); full price

The third and final collaboration between Mozart and Da Ponte was first performed just eight years after Pierre Choderlos de Laclos published *Les liaisons dangereuses*, a novel with which *Così fan tutte* (Women Are Like That) has much in common: both dramatize the disruptive force of sexuality, and both are informed by a distinctly modern spirit of self-awareness. Both, furthermore, have been deplored as scandalous and corrupting creations. The supposed licentiousness of *Così fan tutte* kept it off the stage for much of the nineteenth century (its detractors included Beethoven), and it was not until the 1890s that the opera's star finally begin to ascend. Even now *Così* can leave audiences unsettled: its themes of faith and trust remain unresolved at the opera's close, and no-one leaves a performance thinking that a happy ending or a rosy future lies ahead of the protagonists.

The plot, which Da Ponte for once devised himself, has the perfection of farce. Ferrando and Guglielmo are convinced of the fidelity of Fiordiligi and Dorabella, sisters to whom they are engaged. Don Alfonso, a friend, believes all women are fickle and wagers he can prove it. Ferrando and Guglielmo pretend to enlist in the army, but they return disguised as Albanians and proceed to court each other's fiancée. Each woman succumbs to her new lover's advances. Having lost the bet, Ferrando and Guglielmo "return" and confront Fiordiligi and Dorabella. Having received apologies, they pay Alfonso his money and forgive the sisters their deceit.

The structural symmetries of Da Ponte's plot inspired Mozart to write some of his most beautiful music, creating the most perfect ensemble opera ever written. This is not to say that there are no arias or big tunes (every lead has one aria in each of the two acts), but above all else *Così* demands six singers who can play their roles as part of a greater whole – if any one role dominates, the opera simply doesn't work. Though the story is farcical, Mozart's music is largely serious, and all the better for that. In Act I, for example, when Fiordiligi, Dorabella and Alfonso bid farewell to Ferrando and Guglielmo with "Soave sia il vento" (May the wind be gentle), Mozart creates a trio of melancholy pathos in which the gentle string accompaniment imitates the breezes to which the women refer in their farewell. References to this mournful music crop up throughout the two acts (significantly so during "the return"), and Mozart's use of similarly repeated themes contributes to the opera's complex structure, in which harmony, tonality and deployment of instruments add much to the cohesion of the opera. You might not consciously perceive it, but Mozart's inspired use of thematic references, snatches of melody and orchestration (prominent bassoon for comedy, horn for more serious episodes) links the opera's scenes and ideas like a daisy-chain. Analysis reveals *Così* to be one of Mozart's most remarkable creations, but you don't need to be a musician to be amazed by the finale, in which the opera's disparate musical components are – like the lovers themselves – brought together in a conclusion that seems completely natural.

René Jacobs' 1999 period-instrument recording is the freshest interpretation for many years. The singing is faultless throughout, with probably as fine a Mozart cast as can be assembled anywhere today, and Jacobs provides light, intelligent and imaginative support. The three CDs come with a multimedia CD Rom (formatted for both PC and Mac) that includes not only the complete opera, but also a full libretto (with translations) plus essays and features on Mozart, *Così* and the opera's historical background.

55

Wolfgang Amadeus Mozart

Die Zauberflöte

Evelyn Lear (Pamina), Roberta Peters (Queen of the Night), Fritz
Wunderlich (Tamino), Dietrich Fischer-Dieskau (Papageno), Franz Crass
(Sarastro); Berlin RIAS Chamber Choir; Berlin Philharmonic Orchestra; Karl
Böhm (conductor)

Deutsche Grammophon 449 749-2GOR2; 2 CDs; mid-price

Of all Mozart's operas, *Die
Zauberflöte* (The Magic Flute) is
by some way the strangest. On
the one hand it's a story of lovers
in jeopardy, as transparent and
light as a pantomime; on the
other, it's an opaque allegory that
has occasioned reams of interpre-
tative speculation. The project
was suggested by Emanuel
Schikaneder, an actor-singer-impresario whom Mozart came to
know through their membership of the same Viennese Masonic
lodge. Something of a chancer, Schikaneder was facing a spell in
a debtor's prison and turned to Mozart to write a piece for his
latest last-ditch venture, the Theater auf der Wieden. Since his
company was made up of singing actors rather than acting
singers, it was agreed that Mozart should compose a *Singspiel* and
that, to save money, Schikaneder should write the libretto. With
both eyes on the box office they settled on a fairy tale,
Liebeskind's "Lulu, oder Die Zauberflöte", for their source.

Very simply, the plot concerns two couples – Prince Tamino
and Pamina; Papageno and Papagena – who are eventually united after various trials; the men's success in these trials also gains
them acceptance into Sarastro's Temple brotherhood, and brings
about the ruin of the evil duo of the Queen of the Night
(Pamina's mother) and Monostatos (Sarastro's servant). The

Masons of Mozart's Vienna saw themselves as a philosophical association persecuted by the empress Maria Theresa, her Habsburg state and the Catholic Church. With this in mind *Zauberflöte*'s plot takes on a new complexion: the Queen is Maria Theresa, the thuggish Monostatos represents the Church, the wise and beneficent Sarastro is the Viennese scientist and prominent Mason Ignaz von Born, and each of the remaining characters embodies various aspects of Masonic idealism. At least, that is the most likely interpretation. A Masonic subtext is suggested by the prevalence of the number three in such guises as the opera's dominant key (E flat, which has three flats), the three chords that introduce the Three Ladies and the Three Boys, and the three trials overseen by the three priests.

Ultimately, though, the esoteric meaning of *Die Zauberflöte* is less important than the overt subject matter, which is conveyed through a consistently entertaining mix of popular tunes, high-art arias, solemn Gluck-like drama and bel canto display. As with Mozart's *Die Entführung*, the style veers rapidly from one extreme to the other, ranging from hieratic drama to knockabout comedy in the space of a few minutes. And within that range lies some of the finest vocal music Mozart ever produced, from heartfelt love songs (Tamino's love-at-first-sight outpouring) to outrageously silly exchanges (Papageno's duet with Papagena, in which they sing "Pa-pa-pa-pa" some 48 times) and hair-raising coloratura dementia (the Queen of the Night's murderous, and murderously difficult, showpieces).

Surprisingly, considering his reputation as a humourless taskmaster, Karl Böhm was one of the finest conductors of *Zauberflöte*, and his second recording, for Deutsche Grammophon, is a gem. Not only does he balance the pacing and structure perfectly, but he was also fortunate in having one of the century's greatest Mozart casts. Wunderlich's Tamino is honeyed and lithe, Franz Crass is the most convincing Sarastro on record, Friedrich Lenz is a characterful Monostatos, and Fischer-Dieskau's Papageno is one of his great successes as an operatic singer. On top of this, Roberta Peters is an electrifyingly powerful Queen of the Night – indeed, Evelyn Lear's workaday Pamina is the only real weakness.

56

Modest Mussorgsky

Boris Godounov

Nikolai Putilin / Vladimir Vaneev (Boris Godounov), Viktor Lutsuk / Vladimir Galusin (Grigory), Nikolai Ohotnikov (Pimen), Konstantin Pluzhnikov (Shuisky); Kirov Opera Chorus and Orchestra; Valery Gergiev (conductor)

Philips 462 230-2; 5 CDs; mid-price

Mussorgsky was Russian opera's great outsider, for reasons that are not difficult to locate: his alcoholism made him aggressive and unreliable; he had almost no training; and he wrote music that few, if any, understood. Rimsky-Korsakov, for example, dismissed *Boris Godounov* for its "absurd, ugly part-writing, sometimes strikingly illogical modulation [and] unsuccessful orchestration". Yet these very qualities were at the heart of Mussorgsky's unique musical personality. Contemptuous of his contemporaries' weakness for emptily beautiful music, he saw his responsibility as being to illuminate the lives and history of his people – "Music a means of communication," he wrote, "not an end in itself."

The gestation of this extraordinary piece was tortuous. Mussorgsky completed his first version in 1869, only to realize that, with a cast dwarfed by its title role and no leading female part, he could get no interest from the theatres. Two years later he revised it, broadening the cast, the narrative and the score until, in 1872, he produced what was, in essence, a new opera. The draft adhered much more closely to the Pushkin story from which the opera is derived, charting the downfall of Tsar Boris, who assumes the throne after murdering the rightful heir, Dimitry. Racked by guilt, Boris confesses his crime to the novice monk Grigory, who leaves for Poland where, now claiming he is

Dimitry, he raises an army. Boris slowly descends into madness and, after confessing his sins to God, dies.

After Mussorgsky's death in 1881, Rimsky-Korsakov carried out an "improvement" of the score, which remained in circulation until the 1970s, when Mussorgsky's 1872 edition supplanted it in the repertoire. Rimsky-Korsakov acted out of the best intentions, for Mussorgsky's final edition is a bleak creation, in which the tormented characters are starkly delineated in tableau-like scenes, each of which is linked through the use of recurring motifs. The vocal style is austere and uningratiating; there are no arias, and most of the melodies are so long that they seem to have neither a beginning nor an end. Mussorgsky fused the metre of spoken Russian and the intervals of native folk song, merging them in a style of his own invention (*glukho*), a sung speech that requires the singer to blur the written line by exaggerating certain syllables to emphasize the meaning of the text. This may not sound much like fun, but the orchestral and choral background of this opera is so theatrical, and the steady development of tension so intense, that *Boris Godounov* is hypnotically absorbing.

Towering above the narrative is the demonic presence of Boris, who, together with the omnipresent chorus, permeates the whole opera. Even though Mussorgsky ended up giving him just two major episodes – the famously noisy coronation scene in Act I (renowned for its pealing bells and massed chorus), and his thirty-minute death scene – he is the summit of the bass repertoire, and even if little of his music is particularly memorable, you are left with an incredibly vivid perception of the character.

Valery Gergiev's 1998 recording of *Boris* is terrific value: it contains both editions in a five-disc box that sells for the price of three CDs. Both performances are astonishingly powerful, but the later version has the edge for Vladimir Vaneev's resonantly physical portrayal of the title role, and the dramatic tenor Vladimir Galusin's sensational performance as Grigory. Gergiev's conducting is highly disciplined, and his swift tempi and instrumental articulation bring much-needed shape to Mussorgsky's rambling epic. The orchestra and chorus play their hearts out, and the sound is electrifying.

57

Jacques Offenbach

Orphée aux Enfers

Michel Sénéchal (Orphée), Mady Mesplé (Eurydice), Charles Burles (Jupiter); Toulouse Capitole Chorus and Orchestra; Michel Plasson (conductor)

EMI CDS7 49647-2; 2 CDs; full price

The extravagant and repressive Napoleon III was subjected to almost continual ridicule by caricaturists and writers, but France's most popular satirist during the Second Empire was Jacques Offenbach, the man who made operetta an international art form, thereby paving the way for Lehár, Sullivan and the musicals of the twentieth century. His career began slowly, and not until 1855, when he started presenting seasons of his operettas in a small theatre on the Champs-Elysées, did his fortunes change. *Orphée aux Enfers* (Orpheus in the Underworld), was especially successful, so much so that even Napoleon was won over – within eighteen months of the premiere he requested a command performance, after which he personally congratulated the composer. Conservative critics, however, were appalled by the cynicism of Offenbach's work (one of the qualities that has kept it fresh), and by his treatment of certain venerated composers – there was a highly public battle between Offenbach and one Jules Janin, who attacked Offenbach's mocking of Gluck's "Che farò senza Euridice" (from *Orfeo ed Euridice* – see p.62) as a "desecration".

For their assault on the Second Empire's predilection for neo-classical pomposity, Offenbach and his librettist Ludovic Halévy retained nothing but the bare outline of the story as told in Gluck's hallowed opera: Orpheus travels to Hades to retrieve

Eurydice from Pluto, but looks back on the way out of the underworld and a result loses her. But in this version Orpheus is a talentless fool who is desperate to get rid of Eurydice, who is a nagging trollop. Public opinion is pitted against the bored and feckless gods (caricatures of members of the government), the boss of whom, Jupiter (ie Napoleon), is derided for everything from his ugliness and stupidity to his profligacy and roving eye.

When it came to setting Halévy's libretto Offenbach created a score almost unique in operetta in that there are no tedious episodes, no flat jokes and no limp melodies – everything from the overture to the concluding bacchanal in Hades is irrepressibly vivacious. The best-known episode is of course the "galop infernal", universally known as the "can can" – "at last something you can dance to" sing the revellers at the farewell party for the gods. The energy of this music is dazzling, and although it occupies no more than two of the work's hundred minutes, it is characteristic of the overall élan of *Orphée*. There are many other fantastic orchestral effects, such as Jupiter's "buzzing" transformation into a fly and Pluto's explosive entrance in Act II, and a number of the more extended solos have entered the repertoire of recital songs – notably John Styx's "Quand j'étais roi de Béotie" (When I was King of the Beotians). Each of the fourteen lead roles is granted at least one show-tune, in parodic styles that run the gamut from Mozart to Wagner, with the odd swipe at more populist music along the way – Orpheus's poor musicianship, for example, is illustrated by his playing an excerpt from Strauss's "Skater Waltz").

In this 1978 recording Michel Plasson brilliantly captures the wild decadence of *Orphée*. Mady Mesplé is splendidly outré as Eurydice, making the most of her sighing over the irresistible Aristeus, Michel Sénéchal's Orpheus is the soul of artistic pretension, and the show is all but stolen by Charles Burles's degenerate Jupiter. The ensemble numbers rip along, and the orchestra provide a richly coloured background, with the fruity wind section and booming percussion especially boisterous during the can can. The engineers have captured the performance in warm and generous sound.

Jacques Offenbach

Les Contes d'Hoffmann

Raoul Jobin (Hoffmann), Renée Doria (Olympia), Vina Bovy (Giulietta); Paris Opéra-Comique Chorus and Orchestra; André Cluytens (conductor)

EMI CMS5 65260-2; 2 CDs; mid-price

In 1875, after his latest theatrical venture had left him almost bankrupt, Offenbach realized that few of his operettas had survived the change in taste that followed France's defeat by the Prussian army in 1871, and that as a composer in his fifties his prospects were less than rosy. He attempted to establish himself in the United States, but after almost eighteen months of failure he concluded that the most effective way of securing his place in posterity was to write a full-blown opera to rival the work of Gounod, Saint-Saëns and Bizet (whose *Carmen* had begun to draw in the crowds shortly before Offenbach's emigration). *Les Contes d'Hoffmann* (The Tales of Hoffmann) occupied Offenbach intermittently for the last three years of his life, but he would not live to see its success: it remained incomplete until Ernst Guiraud filled out the sketches in readiness for the first production, at the Opéra-Comique in January 1881, four months after Offenbach's death.

The composer was fortunate in securing a libretto from the famed partnership of Barbier and Carré, whose dark and witty text lent itself to Offenbach's left-of-centre talent. The three central acts (framed by a Prologue and Epilogue) recount three tales by Ernst Theodor Hoffmann (1776–1822), a celebrated German writer, composer and critic. The first concerns an inventor and his mechanical doll, Olympia, by whom Hoffmann is seduced; the second involves another of Hoffmann's passions, Antonia, a consumptive singer who falls prey to the evil Dr Miracle; and the third tells of Giulietta, who tries to trick Hoffmann into selling his soul.

Hoffmann was Offenbach's first and last opera, in that it was his only through-composed work without spoken dialogue, but it is a close relative of his other stage works, as he simply adapted his operetta style to fit the more sombre tone of the libretto. Offenbach's trademark wit is in evidence throughout, but it plays a relieving rather than a defining role, so that music-hall episodes such as Olympia's coloratura "mechanical" aria, in which her voice drops in a huge glissando from high above the stave every time her mechanism runs low, serve to leaven the menace of the inventor's rival, Coppélius. Similarly, the comic minor character Frantz, who in Act IV fails to reach the notes at the end of his scales (a parody of a real tenor who was then past his prime) is an entertaining diversion in an act dominated by minor-key music, stentorian outbursts and a darkly coloured atmosphere, such as the apparently gentle but superbly ominous "Barcarole" that opens the act. *Hoffmann*'s distinguishing quality is melancholia (the hero ends the opera despairing and loveless), yet there are so many showpieces for Hoffmann's tenor and the three female leads (often played by one singer but scored for coloratura, lyric and dramatic sopranos) that it never becomes maudlin.

Capturing *Hoffmann*'s balance between light and darkness on record is not easy, but one set, recorded in 1948, gauges the work's constantly changing hue to perfection. French music was the forte of French conductor André Cluytens, and his performance for EMI has a cohesion unique on record. He knew each of his cast from many years' work together on stage in Paris, and he had conducted Raoul Jobin in the title role on more than fifty occasions before taking it to the studio. Doria's witty Olympia and Bovy's seductive Giulietta are outstanding, but the whole cast, the superbly drilled chorus and the gloriously fruity orchestra contribute to a recording which, fifty years on, is still without rival.

59

Amilcare Ponchielli

La Gioconda

Anita Cerquetti (Gioconda), Mario del Monaco (Enzo), Ettore Bastianini (Barnaba), Giulietta Simionato (Laura); MMF Chorus and Orchestra; Gianandrea Gavazzeni (conductor)

Decca 433 770–2DMO2; 2 CDs; mid-price

Such was the demand for new operas in nineteenth-century Italy that hundreds of composers were given the opportunity to write for the stage. So comprehensive was Verdi's dominance during the middle-to-late years of the century, however, that all but a handful of his contemporaries rapidly fell into deep obscurity. Of this handful, perhaps the best known is Amilcare Ponchielli, whose name has survived thanks to a single opera.

Unlike Verdi, Ponchielli was a child prodigy, and he was enrolled at the Milan Conservatory shortly before his tenth birthday. Having graduated, he made the mistake of returning to his birthplace near Cremona, and while his works achieved local popularity they were almost completely ignored in Italy's major musical centres. Eventually, in 1872, he was commissioned to provide a work for La Scala, Milan. This led to a publishing contract and, in 1876, a partnership with Boito (Verdi's great librettist), who provided him with a text based on Victor Hugo's tragic tale of the seventeenth-century Venetian street-singer La Gioconda. First performed in 1876, the eponymous opera was a massive hit, but neither of his last two operas survived their time, and he devoted the remaining ten years of his life to teaching at the Milan Conservatory, where his pupils included Puccini and Mascagni.

La Gioconda is the epitome of romantic melodrama. Gioconda is pursued by Barnaba who, when rejected, denounces her mother, La Cieca, as a witch. When Cieca is attacked the mysterious fisherman Enzo and the Inquisitor Alvise save her life. Gioconda falls in love with Enzo, unaware that he and Alvise's wife, Laura, used to be lovers. Barnaba tricks Alvise into believing that his wife is having an affair with Enzo. Alvise tries to poison Laura and then, believing her to be dead, celebrates with a banquet. Enzo attacks Alvise and is arrested. Barnaba then promises Gioconda that he will save Enzo – but only if she will yield to his advances; but Enzo escapes, leaving Gioconda to Barnaba. Rather than submit, Gioconda commits suicide.

Considering *La Gioconda's* reputation as a vocal tour de force, it is ironic that the opera's best-known music is the ballet "Dance of the Hours", an exquisite divertissement regularly heard in concert halls. This episode, like so much else in the opera, is typical of *Gioconda's* indebtedness to Verdi, in particular to Verdi's absorption of the spectacular theatricality of French Grand Opéra. The mighty choruses – famously the massed shout that brings Act III to its thunderous climax – are all about achieving maximum gallery-pleasing effect, as is Ponchielli's way of juxtaposing long and powerful vocal lines against sudden, impassioned bursts of dialogue, creating an ebb and flow comparable to that of works such as *La Forza del Destino* (see p.177). Nowhere is this juxtaposition more impressive than in Act II, where Enzo's ardent "Cielo e mar"(Heaven and sea) is followed by his shirt-tearing duet with Laura, a sequence that's one of the highlights of all romantic Italian opera.

Callas's 1959 performance for EMI is rightly famous, but this Decca recording, made two years earlier, has a stronger all-round cast and greater musical consistency. Anita Cerquetti was at her peak, and she gives a gloriously impassioned portrayal of the title role. For a change, Mario del Monaco does not shout, but gives a rounded, human performance as Enzo. Bastianini's huge baritone might have been created for Barnaba, and he clearly had a great time recording it. Simionato is vocally sumptuous as Laura, and in her duet with del Monaco the music takes flight as on no other recording. The whole is tightly conducted and warmly recorded.

60

Sergei Prokofiev

The Love for Three Oranges

Gabriel Bacquier (King of Clubs), Jules Bastin (Cook), Jean-Luc Viala (Prince), Catherine Dubosc (Ninetta); Lyon Opera Chorus and Orchestra; Kent Nagano (conductor)

Virgin VCD7 59566-2; 2 CDs; full price

Of the eight operas that Prokofiev completed, the most accessible is the opera-within-an-opera *The Love for Three Oranges*, a delightfully surreal satire of operatic convention (amongst other things) based on a play by the eighteenth-century comic playwright Carlo Gozzi, whose *Turandot* would serve as the basis for Puccini's last opera (see p.127). Taking his libretto from theatre director Vsevolod Meyerhold's French translation of Gozzi's *L'Amore delle tre Melarance*, Prokofiev created an engagingly lunatic world peopled by "Monsters, Drunkards, Gluttons, Guards, Servants, Soldiers, Jokers, Highbrows, Wits, Romantics, Lowbrows, Little Devils, Doctors and Courtiers".

Meyerhold's theories on "the diminution of the role of the actor" and the need to "challenge conventional audience relationships" had a strong influence on Prokofiev's anti-naturalistic treatment of Gozzi's play. Inevitably, he made numerous alterations to the original, but the elements are unchanged. The King of Clubs fears that his sickly son, the Prince, is going to die. His advisers tell him that the only cure is laughter. Various amusements are attempted, all of which fail, but then the witch Fata Morgana accidentally "cures" the Prince by falling over and making him laugh. As revenge for her humiliation, she curses the Prince: he will fall in love with three oranges, in search of which he will spend the rest of his life. However, while trawling through the desert he finds the oranges, each of which contains a princess: the first two die of thirst, but the third, Ninetta, survives to join the Prince on his return home.

Musically, *The Love for Three Oranges* is something of an amalgam of a rhythmically driven, almost martial sound-world (the opera's famous March and Scherzo are the best known examples) and the more refined, neo-classical world of his *Symphony No. 1*. These very different aspects of the composer's musical psyche are brilliantly synthesized, and the score perfectly captures the surreal frenzy of the drama. As a general means of reference Prokofiev uses diatonic music to represent the forces of good and chromatic music for evil, but each of the characters – many of whom give the impression of having wandered in from other operas – is precisely delineated through the score, and everyone and everything is tagged through the use of leitmotif. Except for Ninetta's lyrical outpourings, the vocal writing is subjugated to the metre of the text in a manner that makes the writing fragmented and brittle. Consequently, short, acerbic phrases predominate to such an extent that *Love for Three Oranges* favours the casting of singing actors, rather than of singers who are able to act. This jumpy, unstable nature of the vocal score contributes to the opera's curiously cinematic feel, notably in the rapidity of scene, key and tempo changes; indeed, the final scene, in which the entire cast chase each other around the stage to music of manic contrapuntal virtuosity, is an outright parody of the Hollywood silent movies to which Prokofiev was introduced while finishing the score in America.

This award-winning performance, issued in 1989, was one of the most notable opera recordings of the decade. Played and sung by a French company who have learnt the work in repertoire, it has a palpable unity of intent and Nagano perfectly judges the character of the farce, never over-playing it, but nonetheless allowing his cast to enjoy themselves. His direction is precise and ideally paced, and although on occasions there is a tendency to exaggerate the more aggressive episodes, he is remarkably successful in bridging the stylistic jumps. His singers are outstanding and the recording is a model of clarity and balance.

Giacomo Puccini

La Bohème

Renata Tebaldi (Mimi), Carlo Bergonzi (Rodolfo), Gianna d'Angelo
(Musetta), Ettore Bastianini (Marcello); Santa Cecilia Academy Chorus and
Orchestra; Tullio Serafin (conductor)

Decca 448 725-2DF2; 2 CDs; mid-price

Puccini was introduced to Henry Murger's novel *La vie de Bohème* by Leoncavallo (see p.83), who was at the time himself working on an operatic adaptation of the book. Puccini decided to have a go himself, which led to a public battle over the rights to Murger's work – a battle won by Puccini, since he was the first to the finishing line, completing his score in 1895. The luscious score, vivid characterization and lachrymose storyline of *La Bohème* ensured that within six months of its premiere it had become Puccini's most popular work. Nowadays it's not just the best-known of his creations – it's one of the world's three or four most frequently performed operas.

Puccini's librettists, Giuseppe Giacosa and Luigi Illica, milked the story for every last drop of sentiment. The poet Rodolfo and the painter Marcello share a garret in which they work at their art in noble indifference to their squalid conditions and unremitting poverty. Rodolfo falls in love with Mimi, a consumptive seamstress, whom he introduces to his friends, including the philosopher Colline and Musetta, one of Marcello's old flames, with whom Marcello once again falls in love. Weeks pass and Rodolfo abandons Mimi, since he can no longer bear the pain of life with a terminally ill girlfriend, but when Mimi's end draws near Rodolfo returns just in time to confess his undying love.

From the opening ensemble the opera is dominated by an astonishing melodic richness, as the big-hitting arias rise with great dramatic impact from the fast-moving "conversational" dialogue. From the bustling camaraderie of the bohemians in Act I emerge two of the most popular operatic songs ever written: Rodolfo's "Che gelida manina" (Your tiny hand is frozen), and Mimi's rejoinder "Mi, chiamano Mimi" (They call me Mimi). These two arias, recalled through the repetition of motifs or more subtle echoes, tie the opera together in a way that distinguishes a Puccini creation from the more basic assembly techniques of many of his contemporaries. The most conspicuous difference between *Bohème* and the style of *verismo* opera, however, lies in the quality of the vocal lines. For example, when the coquettish Musetta is introduced during the opening of Act II, she announces herself through an erotic cantilena, "Quando me'n vo" (When I walk out), that could almost be a song by Bellini, although it's framed by a frantic ensemble that could only be Puccini's.

The long-suffering Marcello, the vampish Musetta, the capricious Rodolfo and the fragile, guileless Mimi have more substance than the customary *verismo* crew, and even the blustering Benoit and the philosophical Colline (who sings a famous song to his coat in the final act) are well-defined musical personalities. The audience's engagement with Puccini's protagonists gives the final tragedy a poignancy unmatched by any other Italian opera of the period. The sense of loss and of the belated onset of responsibility is heightened by music in which the material first heard in Act I returns as a reminiscence of earlier happiness. Only the hardest of hearts could remain untouched.

Of the three dozen recordings of *La Bohème* there is one clear leader. Taped in 1958, Tullio Serafin's performance with the Santa Cecilia Academy stands out for its integrity, Serafin's vital conducting and its peerless cast – with the young Carlo Bergonzi in wonderfully elegant form as Rodolfo, Renata Tebaldi a mature but touching Mimi and Ettore Bastianini a likable, vocally sumptuous Marcello. The supporting cast are uniformly excellent and the fine orchestra and warmly balanced early stereo recording add to the enduring appeal of this classic performance.

62

Giacomo Puccini

Tosca

Maria Callas (Floria Tosca), Giuseppe di Stefano (Mario Cavaradossi), Tito Gobbi (Scarpia), Franco Calabrese (Angelotti); La Scala Chorus and Orchestra; Victor de Sabata (conductor)

EMI CDS5 56304-2; 2 CDs; full price

Benjamin Britten once spoke of being "sickened by the cheapness and emptiness" of *Tosca*, while the critic Joseph Kermann famously dismissed it as a "shabby little shocker". But there is a sincerity to Puccini's shallowness that redeems even the cheapest theatrical trick – and music this tuneful is difficult to resist. Certainly the general opera-going public has had few problems with *Tosca*. The first performance in 1900 was a hit with the Rome audience, and those critics who were scandalized by Puccini's sexual explicitness merely fanned the flames of its notoriety, guaranteeing the composer his second international success.

Tosca is propelled by the dynamics of the relationships between its three central characters. Cavaradossi, a painter, protects his friend Angelotti, an escaped political prisoner, from the forces of the evil Baron Scarpia. Floria Tosca, a fiery singer with whom the artist is having a relationship, unwittingly leads Scarpia's men to Cavaradossi, who is tortured for information on Angelotti. Scarpia promises Tosca that he will release him if she yields to him. She agrees, but while Scarpia pretends to write the release order she stabs him to death. Awaiting execution, Cavaradossi is joined by Tosca, who tells him that Scarpia promised to replace the soldiers' bullets with blanks; but no such order was made and Cavaradossi is shot dead. Distraught, Tosca throws herself to her death off the palace walls.

Opera has no more monstrous figure than Scarpia, whose motif is announced in the work's forbidding opening chords. Incapable of finding pleasure except in conquest, Scarpia is a depraved sadist who delights in proclaiming his own depravity – his twisted "Credo" at the close of Act I thunderously states his case as he broods on his lust for Tosca and fantasizes about Cavaradossi's bloody execution. The tension is heightened by the accompaniment of a *Tè Deum*, to which he eventually joins his voice before a tumultuous orchestral explosion brings the act to an end. With the "Credo" finished he has no further arias, but rather a string of thickly accompanied arioso passages in which the instrumentation and harmony conjure a sense of evil comparable to the characterization of Hagen in Wagner's *Götterdämmerung*.

Scarpia's relationship with Tosca is the axis upon which the drama spins, but their exchanges are almost entirely confined to the second act. With the exception of Cavaradossi's "Vittoria!", a heart-stopping denunciation of Scarpia, and Tosca's sole aria, the brief but harrowing "Vissi d'arte" (I lived for art), this act is given over to the morbid, quasi-ritualistic duel between heroine and anti-hero, in which Puccini sustains a tension between Scarpia's long, minatory phrases and Tosca's rapid, apprehensive interjections. The outer acts conform more closely to the traditional "numbers" structure, rather like *La Bohème*, with two major arias for Cavaradossi and two exquisite duets for Cavaradossi and Tosca.

Victor de Sabata's 1953 recording of *Tosca* justifiably remains one of the most famous operatic recordings. It demonstrates exactly why the conductor's name continues to inspire such reverence: the feeling for structure and momentum is uncanny, while his awareness of detail gives every motif and phrase its proper emphasis. Maria Callas was in her prime, and hers is the most powerful portrayal of Tosca on record. Gobbi defined Scarpia for every subsequent interpreter of the role, and he remains the nastiest Scarpia there has ever been. The only real weakness, and then a slight one, is di Stefano's Cavaradossi, who strains his delicate tenor to compete with the high-octane singing from Callas and Gobbi. Regardless of this quibble, and the mono sound, this is a definitive Puccini recording.

63

Giacomo Puccini

Madama Butterfly

Renata Tebaldi (Butterfly), Carlo Bergonzi (Pinkerton), Enzo Sordello (Sharpless), Fiorenzo Cossotto (Suzuki); Santa Cecilia Academy Chorus and Orchestra; Tullio Serafin (conductor)

Decca 425 531-2DM2; 2 CDs; mid-price

With good reason Puccini expected his fifth opera, *Madama Butterfly*, to score another triumph. *La Bohème* and *Tosca* were well established in the repertoire, and the personnel engaged for the premiere in 1904 could not have been bettered. But Puccini's enemies bought up many of the theatre's seats and the first performance was booed and heckled so loudly it was nearly abandoned. Although Puccini blamed his enemies for the flop, he privately accepted that the two acts were too long, and that by failing to provide even a single aria for the tenor he had been asking for trouble. He revised the score, breaking the second act into two, cutting a considerable amount of music and providing a tenor aria for Act III. At its premiere just three months later the revision was hailed a masterpiece and Puccini was, again, Italy's number one composer.

Giacosa and Illica's libretto, based on a true story, tells of a sixteen-year-old Japanese girl (Butterfly) who marries a visiting American sailor and bears him a child, only to be abandoned when he returns to America and his American wife. Her tragedy is compounded when several years later he returns, accompanied by his wife, to claim the young boy. Rather than live with the shame, Butterfly kills herself. The character of Butterfly gives plenty of ammunition to Puccini's detractors: this is the "weaker" sex at its weakest, and she embodies some thoroughly distasteful racial attitudes. However, the power of the music, intensity of the drama, and Butterfly's transition from ingenuous youth to melancholy maturity within the space of just two hours are sufficiently engrossing to distract from the underlying misogyny.

Along the way lies some intensely poignant music – notably the famous "Un bel dì" (One fine day) – but the highlight of the whole opera is Butterfly's moment of bliss, her Act I duet with Pinkerton, "Bimba, bimba, dagli occhi pieni di malia" (Dear child, with bewitching eyes). Lasting nearly a quarter of an hour, the duet begins with delicate exchanges and builds towards a series of tremendous unison phrases that culminate in a shared high C of rapturous devotion. Pinkerton himself is at first all bluster and bonhomie, traits signalled by lusty quotations from "The Star Spangled Banner" (just as Butterfly and her family are tagged with music that uses the oriental-sounding pentatonic scale). It doesn't take long, however, for him to emerge in his true colours as a self-righteous egoist, whose primary interest in Butterfly is utterly basic – as he gloats to Sharpless, the marriage agreement is not even binding. Callously detached from the suffering he causes, Pinkerton is assigned music that resembles that of the standard Italian romantic tenor lead, an incongruity that intensifies his cruelty. Unlike the traditional tenor lead, however, he gets only one set-piece aria, "Addio fiorito asil" (Farewell, blossoming refuge), which comes shortly before the end.

The brief partnership of Renata Tebaldi and Carlo Bergonzi on the Decca label between 1958 and 1960 produced some of the finest Italian opera recordings ever made. Tebaldi rarely suggests the fragility of a sixteen-year-old, but she comes into her own during the final act, when the weight of her voice is more in keeping with the gravity of her situation. Bergonzi was famed for his tasteful musicianship, but in his prime he was not above stooping to the odd burst of vulgarity, and his portrayal of Pinkerton is truly horrible, albeit beautifully horrible. Serafin is in nimble form, and he draws some glorious playing from the Santa Cecilia Academy Chorus and Orchestra.

64

Giacomo Puccini

Turandot

Birgit Nilsson (Turandot), Franco Corelli (Calaf), Renata Scotto (Liù); Rome
Opera Chorus and Orchestra; Giuseppe Molinari-Pradelli (conductor)

EMI CMS7 69327-2; 2 CDs; full price

In 1911 Puccini saw a performance in Berlin of Gozzi's play *Turandot* in a production which so impressed him that he decided there and then to turn it into an opera. Eight years were to pass, however, before he got round to it, a delay caused by Puccini's throat cancer, his severe demands on his librettists and by his own regular crises of confidence. At one point, he is said to have remarked to Giuseppe Adami (one of his librettists): "My opera will be staged incomplete, and then someone will come onto the stage and say to the public: 'At this point the composer died.'" As things turned out, that's exactly what happened. Puccini's cancer killed him in 1924, nearly five years into *Turandot's* gestation, and he left the final act incomplete. The little-known composer Franco Alfano was brought in to finish the job and, all things considered, he did remarkably well; but the conductor of the premiere, Arturo Toscanini, thought otherwise. When the performance reached the point where Alfano took over, he lowered his baton and announced to the Milanese audience: "At this point the master died."

Reaction to the new work was generally flattering, although some were, again, alarmed by the composer's fondness for females in extreme distress. The source of this distress, Princess Turandot, opens the opera by announcing that she will marry whoever can answer her three riddles. Failure will result in death, and many duly fail. Prince Calaf answer the riddles correctly, however, but turns the tables on Turandot by promising to walk to the executioner's block if she can guess his name before sunrise the following day. The Princess then threatens to put the people to death if they fail to reveal the stranger's name. Calaf's adoring admirer, Liù, comes forward and announces that she alone knows it, but rather than betray him she takes her own life. Shortly before dawn Calaf confronts Turandot with his love and tells her his name; she in turn announces that the stranger's name is love and they fall into each other's arms.

Turandot is one of the vilest creations in all opera, and – as with Scarpia – you can't help feeling that Puccini revelled in the creation of this deeply repellent character, just as he lavished some of the opera's finest music on the hapless Liù. But the decadent luxuriousness of Puccini's music goes a long way to camouflage the composer's dubious morality. Indeed, *Turandot* is the operatic equivalent of bathing in champagne, so rich and sensual are the tunes and orchestration. Best known is Calaf's haunting "Nessun dorma" (None shall sleep), but this is far from being an isolated highlight: Calaf's "Non pangiere, Liù" (Don't weep, Liù) and his answers to the riddles are hair-raisingly exciting, while Turandot's icy "In questa reggia" (In this domain) is among the finest dramatic soprano showpieces ever written. However, the most scintillating episode of the opera is the final love duet, in which Puccini evidently intended to pull out all the stops.

This celebrated recording was made four years after Corelli and Nilsson headed the Met's first revival of *Turandot* for thirty years, and their performances were responsible for bringing the opera wider popularity in the US. Franco Corelli's stupendous, wildly emotional Calaf is the finest ever recorded, and the combination of him and the equally powerful Nilsson produces a performance that beggars description. Molinari-Pradelli might have kept a tighter grip on the reins, but he gets some lovely phrasing and colouring from the orchestra. If you buy just one Puccini opera set, make it this one.

65

Henry Purcell

Dido and Aeneas

Janet Baker (Dido), Raimond Herincx (Aeneas), Patricia Clark (Belinda), Monica Sinclair (Sorceress); St Anthony Singers; English Chamber Orchestra; Anthony Lewis (conductor)

Decca 425 720-2DM; 1 CD; mid-price

Had Henry Purcell lived another fifteen years he would have experienced the London opera mania that was to bring Handel such extraordinary success. As it was, he died having written just one short opera, *Dido and Aeneas*, the first known performance of which, in 1689, was given in the unorthodox surroundings of a girls' school in Chelsea. It's hardly surprising, then, that Purcell is presented as one of the great might-have-beens of opera history, but with *Dido and Aeneas* he created perhaps the greatest of all English-language operas, and the only broadly popular English opera prior to the appearance of Benjamin Britten's *Peter Grimes* (see p.31) in 1945.

Nahum Tate, who adapted his own play *Brutus of Alba* for the libretto, has been ridiculed as a talentless hack ever since Alexander Pope lambasted him in the *Dunciad*. In fact he provides an admirably condensed version of Virgil's story, in which Dido, Queen of Carthage, falls in love with the Trojan prince Aeneas, who ultimately abandons her, driving her to suicide. Tate followed the rules (defined by Dryden) for verses that are to be set to music: namely, that they be short, with frequent stops, repeated lines and not too many consonants. Purcell then provided the finest setting that any librettist could wish for.

Purcell's genius is particularly evident in his recitatives, in which emotional nuance is communicated by an arioso vocalizing of extraordinary subtlety. It can be heard in Dido's recitative "Thy hand, Belinda", which immediately precedes her famous lament, "When I am laid in earth". The recitative is highly chromatic – that is it uses notes foreign to the key that it is in – with the voice moving in a series of small intervals on the syllable "dar" of the word "darkness". The effect is like someone feeling their way in the dark step by step, or, in Dido's case, coming to a true realization of the enormity of her imminent death. The opera is full of such telling details, with the lament having pride of place. This episode has almost talismanic status in English music, and its fame is justified: indeed the single-note repetition of the words "Remember me" must be one of the most agonized and vulnerable moments in the whole of opera.

Aeneas, by comparison with Dido, is psychologically underdeveloped, a characteristic he shares with several operatic heroes. His lack of substance is a far cry from Virgil's noble warrior but it makes Dido's misjudgement of him, and the tragedy that ensues, all the more stark. Equally unlike Virgil is the introduction of malevolent witches as the agents of Dido's destruction (in the *Aeneid* Aeneas is reminded of his duty by the real Mercury). In Tate's restructuring of the story, the witches function as a kind of negative image of Dido and her court, and in fact it is not unknown for Dido and the Sorceress to be played by the same singer. The supernatural had an extremely strong hold over the seventeenth-century imagination, and the Sorceress embodies a powerful tradition, to which Lully's *Armide* (see p.87) also belongs.

Of the many recordings of *Dido* the finest is also one of the earliest. As epitomized by her performance of the closing lament, Janet Baker's attention to the music's emotional substance has never been equalled: there is a fragility to her interpretation that is extraordinarily affecting. She is ably supported by Raimond Herincx, who does his best to inject some life into Aeneas, and Anthony Lewis and the enjoyably old-fashioned ECO provide lively support. The early Decca stereo has been transferred superbly to compact disc.

66

Jean-Philippe Rameau

Hippolyte et Aricie

Veronique Gens (Aricie), Jean-Paul Fouchécourt (Hippolyte), Bernarda Fink (Phèdre), Russell Smythe (Thésée); Sagittarius Ensemble; Les Musiciens du Louvre; Mark Minkowski (conductor)

Archiv 445 853-2; 3 CDs; full price

In Voltaire's words: "After Lully, all other musicians . . . simply imitated him until Rameau came." Rameau's operas did not make a conspicuous break with tradition: their subjects remained myth-bound and involved displays of theatrical opulence, incorporating choruses and ballets. But aspects of his style caused great controversy, notably his predilection for complex counterpoint, his theatrical use of harmony, his lyrical vocal manner and, most importantly, his move towards a smoother manner of construction. The most lasting of his innovations, however, was his cultivation of a highly expressive form of recitative, accompanied by chromatic and colourful orchestral writing. The effect electrified French theatres, and laid the foundation for Gluck's new style (see p.61)

Rameau's first opera, *Hippolyte et Aricie* (Hippolytus and Aricia), diverted a river through the stables of French musical life. Here a heightened dramatic awareness and emotional sensibility were applied to a classical myth in which characterization was unprecedentedly real. The plot, based on the ancient Greek myth first dramatized by Euripides, concentrates on the incestuous love of Phaedra (Phèdre), wife of Theseus (Thésée), for her stepson Hippolytus, the illegitimate son of Theseus. He, however, loves Aricia. Theseus, persuaded that Hippolyte is guilty of assaulting his stepmother, banishes his son, who is then killed by a sea-monster while attempting to escape with Aricia. Phaedra then kills herself, while the exonerated Hippolytus is resurrected and reunited with Aricia.

Aricie, who had played only a minor role in Racine's *Phèdre* – the main source for Abbé Pellegrin's libretto – becomes the drama's pivotal influence in Rameau's opera, while Hippolyte's heroic qualities are displaced by romantic inclinations that, for many contemporaries, were almost too human. Rameau's Phèdre is far more likely to excite sympathy than Racine's, and the part of Thésée was also greatly enhanced – a scene in Hades was interpolated so that Rameau could indulge in some rich character development, and some even richer scene-painting. Thésée leaves the stage a grander and less distant figure than had traditionally been the case.

Spurning convention, Rameau's score illuminates each character as a developing person. Phèdre is initially presented through stringent harmony and arid melody, her character cold and repellent; but with her confession of guilt Rameau's music ripens – the swelling orchestration, the opulent melody and the interjections of a horrified crowd giving her a new magnitude. "Here lies the god of Harmony" read one of Rameau's epitaphs, and Hippolyte abounds with vivid orchestral writing – the storm in Act I and the boiling waters of Act III are among the most gripping episodes in French Baroque opera.

From the opening bars it's easy to hear why the first audience would have found this work shocking: it has a contrapuntal complexity that still sounds daring, and the impression of a restless imagination at work is emphasized by Mark Minkowski's interpretation. Veronique Gens makes a touching Aricie and the tenor Jean-Paul Fouchécourt is a strong Hippolyte. There are times, however, when both seem a little cowed by their orchestral support, but as Phèdre the contralto Bernarda Fink establishes a real sense of a developed characterization, as well as a musical presence that comes to dominate the performance. Archiv's engineers evidently set out to create a distance between the singers and the listener, an effect that is probably closer to a live performance than the airless detachment typical of most studio recording, and the effect is as striking as it is original.

67

Jean-Philippe Rameau

Les Indes galantes

Miriam Ruggeri (Emilie), Howard Crook (Valère/Damon), Bernard Delétré (Huascar/Don Alvar), Jérôme Corréas (Ali), Isabelle Poulenard (L'Amour), Nicolas Rivenq (Osman); Arts Florissants Orchestra and Chorus; William Christie (conductor)

Harmonia Mundi HMC90 1367-9; 3 CDs; full price

After the dramatic excess of *Hippolyte et Aricie* (see p.131) Rameau turned to the lighter vein of opéra-ballet, a fusion of sung narrative and dance. The four dramatic episodes of *Les Indes galantes* (The Amorous Indies), each set in an exotic location, presented the composer with an irresistible challenge to his pictorial skills, a challenge to which he rose with consummate panache, from the volcano in the first episode to the Indian dances of the fourth. However, there's more to *Les Indes galantes* than the conventional special effects of opéra-ballet, for the romances at the heart of Louis Fuzelier's consistently witty libretto gave Rameau an opportunity to cover the full range from light-hearted lyricism to tragedy. Unlike most examples of the genre, this opéra-ballet is populated by living personalities – even the Sun God turns out to be a jealous oaf.

Each of the four parts or Entrées ("The Generous Turk", "The Incas of Peru", "The Flowers" and "The Savages") hinges on a love triangle. The first is set in Turkey and tells of the love between a stranded French couple, Emilie and Valère. The second, set in Peru, concerns a Spanish officer, Don Carlos, who falls in love with an Inca princess, Phani, a passion which so enrages the priest Huascar that he sets off a volcano, inadvertently killing himself and freeing the lovers. Number three is set in Persia, where Prince Tacmas falls in love with Zaïre, a servant of fellow prince Ali, while Tacmas's slave Fatima falls in love with Ali; all is resolved when the princes swap slaves. The final Entrée is set in America, and tells of two officers (one French, Damon, and one Spanish, Don Alvar) who fall in love with the same Native American girl, Zima. Fortunately, she loves her compatriot, Adario, and all ends happily.

The array of ballets, choruses and airs is traditional enough, but Rameau's fluency – with each episode running smoothly into the next – is astounding, and its coherence made *Les Indes galantes* one of Rameau's most widely praised creations (Berlioz was an admirer). The variety of its dance forms, from complex chaconnes to simple minuets, and of its choruses, from laments to the "Brillant Soleil" of Entrée II, makes this opera endlessly entertaining, while Fuzelier's ethnic caricatures illuminate the ways in which non-European culture was perceived during the *ancien régime*. Not all the noble savages are derived from secondhand sources: the final Entrée contains a reworking of Rameau's work for harpsichord "Les sauvages", which was inspired by the appearance of two Native Americans in Paris in 1725.

This is a superb recording. William Christie brings out the music's architecture and vitality, and his team of soloists – all of whom had worked together on a stage production of the opera at the Aix-en-Provence festival in 1991 – are no less alert to the music's energetic, theatrical qualities. Christie's tempi are extremely rapid, but none of his soloists sounds at odds with his overall conception of the work. As Emilie and Valère, the soprano and tenor partnership of Miriam Ruggeri and Howard Crook is one of the performance's highlights, with a perfect fusion of voice-type and temperament. "The Generous Turk" is notable for some marvellous comic touches from Nicolas Rivenq as Osman while "The Flowers" benefits from the delicate pairing of Jérôme Corréas and Jean-Paul Fouchécourt as Ali and Tacmas. "The Savages" is the highlight of the performance, thanks to Christie's driving pace and the indignant rivalry of Crook and Bernard Delétré as Damon and Don Alvar. The orchestra and chorus are excellent throughout.

68

Gioacchino Rossini

L'Italiana in Algeri

Giulietta Simionato (Isabella), Graziella Sciutti (Elvira), Cesare Valletti
(Lindoro), Mario Petri (Mustafà); La Scala Chorus and Orchestra; Carl
Maria Giulini (conductor)

EMI CHS 7 64041 2; 2 CDs; full price

Rossini composed *L'Italiana in
Algeri* (The Italian Girl in
Algiers) as a favour to Cesare
Gallo, the impresario of the cri-
sis-laden Teatro San Benedetto in
Venice, who had been let down
by another composer. With time
short and Gallo increasingly hysterical, Rossini turned to an
established comic libretto (by
Angelo Anelli), commissioned a quick revision and, so it is
claimed, composed the two-and-a-quarter-hour score in twen-
ty-seven days. As Rossini later wrote to a friend, "Nothing
primes inspiration more than necessity, whether it be the presence of a copyist . . . or the prodding of an impresario tearing
his hair. In my time, all the impresarios in Italy were bald at
thirty." *L'Italiana in Algeri* was Rossini's first successful *opera
buffa* (comic opera); one reviewer judged that it was certain to
"find a place among the finest works of genius and art", and
Stendhal declared it to be "perfection . . . as gay as our world is
not."

Anelli's tale is a romantic farce with an exotic setting to give
it some spice. The Bey Mustafà is bored with his wife Elvira
and tells Ali, the captain of his corsairs, to find him a
European wife. The Italian girl Isabella, in search of her lover
Lindoro (who is being held captive by the Bey), is ship-
wrecked, along with her elderly admirer Taddeo, and brought

to Mustafà, who is captivated by her. When Isabella learns of Lindoro's imprisonment she plans their escape by telling the Bey that she wants to make him her "Pappataci", the title given to men who allow their women absolute freedom. As Isabella and Lindoro's ship leaves, Elvira and Mustafà are reunited and all ends happily.

The pacing of this opera is manic and the comedy thoroughly daft – as exemplified by the "sneezing" quintet (part of the Act II escape plan) and the Pappatacci coronation (almost certainly a parody of Masonic induction ceremonies). Yet *L'Italiana* has an undertow of seriousness. Italy had been an occupied nation since the coming of Napoleon (and would remain so after his fall), so Rossini's inclusion of a quote from the "Marseillaise" just before Isabella's inflammatory "Pensa alla patria" (Think of the homeland) was an unambiguously political gesture. The heroine Isabella, scornful of her captors and quicker witted than they, is a figure who would be at home in a more sombre setting, and her music is the opera's most serious and melancholic. That said, the traditions of *commedia dell'arte* lie behind the opera's drastic changes of pace and mood, and in the characterization of the buffoonish Mustafà and idiotic Taddeo you can clearly detect the clowning of Italian street theatre. Their music is full of traditional buffa silliness, including patter songs and wild intervals that leap out of the bass range for which both roles are scored. As for Lindoro, he's an off-the-peg sentimental tenor, but he does have one fine aria, once a favourite of lyric tenors.

Of the many classic Rossini recordings, Carlo Maria Giulini's 1953 performance of *L'Italiana in Algeri* (taped in the wake of a La Scala production) is one of the best. Giulini demonstrates an impeccable feel for shape and gets some sparklingly energetic playing out of the orchestra. The casting is a model of its kind, with Graziella Sciutti a spirited Elvira and Giulietta Simionato a graceful and deliciously sly Isabella. Cesare Valletti's Lindoro is firm but sensitive and the character-bass Mario Petri is in splendid form as Mustafà. The score is cut and the sound is mono, but this is nonetheless a priceless recording.

69

Gioacchino Rossini

Il Barbiere di Siviglia

Maria Callas (Rosina), Luigi Alva (Count Almaviva), Tito Gobbi (Figaro);
Philharmonia Chorus and Orchestra; Alceo Galliera (conductor)

EMI CDS7 47634-8; 2 CDs; mid-price

With the success of *L'Italiana in Algeri* Rossini was well on the way to establishing his dominance of the Italian opera scene, a position he secured by creating nearly forty operas in less than two decades. His impact upon the development of the genre was immense: he was, for example, the first to do away with unaccompanied recitative, thus making the opera a continual musical fabric, and he was the first to write out all the embellishments for his singers, thereby leaving nothing to chance. But the key to his success was sheer tunefulness, a quality which he seemed to achieve with no effort – "Give me a shopping list and I'll set it to music", he once remarked. None of his operas encapsulates his brilliance better than his most consistently popular work – *Il Barbiere di Siviglia* (The Barber of Seville).

Rossini was a keen admirer of Beaumarchais, particularly of *La Barbier de Seville* (1775), a work that had inspired more than twenty operas by the time Rossini came to write his in 1816. The plot involves several of the characters featured in Mozart's *Le Nozze di Figaro* (see p.103) at an earlier stage of their lives. Disguised as a poor student (Lindoro), Count Almaviva is trying to seduce Rosina, the ward of Doctor Bartolo, who wants her for himself. Figaro, the Count's barber and factotum, agrees to help his employer. Bartolo then enlists the support of Don Basilio, a music master, and battle lines are drawn. There follows a series of increasingly madcap episodes, with Almaviva changing disguises and bribing everyone in sight, and Dr Bartolo growing ever more confused. The only constant is Rosina, whose love for Almaviva serves as the axis around which everything else spins.

"The public was completely satisfied," the composer reported after the first performance in 1816, as indeed it was, for the *Barber* is remarkable for what Verdi characterized as an "abundance of true musical ideas". Tuneful, vivacious and inventive in its deployment of the orchestra, *Il Barbiere* is a work of unbelievable energy, especially during the first act, in which nine of the most popular moments in all opera are packed into less than forty minutes of music. This volcanic creativity is harnessed to a scrupulous attention to structure, which maximizes the impact of the musical explosions. The most famous of these is Figaro's riotous Act I aria "Largo al factotum" (Song of the manservant), a virtuosic demonstration of the so-called "Rossini crescendo", whereby tension and release are generated through the repetition of crisply articulated short phrases, which become louder and faster as the aria proceeds. The effect is unique to Rossini, and *Il Barbiere* has a number of examples of it. There are moments of tranquillity too, usually centering on the lovers, though Rosina is for the most part a firecracker of a coloratura mezzo-soprano role. In short, Rossini's opera is a perfect fusion of the elegant wit of Beaumarchais and the knockabout humour of *commedia dell'arte*.

Although Maria Callas was better known for tragedy than comedy, she was responsible for the revival of numerous Rossini comedies, and her voice and personality were ideally suited to the mock-seriousness of Rossini's comic heroines. This is nowhere better demonstrated than on Galliera's celebrated recording of *Il Barbiere*, with Tito Gobbi as Figaro. Callas swoons and swoops her way through Rossini's music in a way that's entirely unique, and her partnership with Gobbi creates a wonderful chemistry. The young Luigi Alva is in fine voice as Almaviva, and Galliera takes a attractively romantic view of the score that sacrifices precision for flair and immediacy.

70

Gioacchino Rossini

La Cenerentola

Teresa Berganza (Cenerentola), Luigi Alva (Don Ramiro), Renato Capecchi (Dandini), Paolo Montarsolo (Don Magnifico); Scottish Opera Chorus; London Symphony Orchestra; Claudio Abbado (conductor)

Deutsche Grammophon 459 448-2; 2 CDs; mid-price

La Cenerentola was another last-minute commission, this time from Pietro Cartoni of Rome's Teatro Valle, who, having had a Rossini libretto banned by the church censors, was in dire need of a substitute. Two days before Christmas 1816, Cartoni summoned Rossini and the writer Jacopo Ferretti to his house, where they discussed "twenty or thirty" possible subjects for a melodrama. Rossini asked Ferretti if he would write him a libretto based on Perrault's *Cinderella*. Ferretti grandly offered to have the draft ready by the morning. At this, Rossini curled up and fell asleep, and when he awoke he found the draft duly finished. The pressure of time meant that certain aspects of the opera, such as the recitative, had to be farmed off to other musicians, and, as was normal with Rossini, the overture was reworked from an earlier opera. But for all the rush, the finished work was a masterpiece, turning Perrault's fairy tale into a touching story of the triumph of love over malice.

The bare bones of *La Cenerentola* are unchanged from its source – Cinderella (Angelina) is exploited by her cruel stepfather (Don Magnifico) and tormented by her horrible stepsisters (Tisbe and Clorinda), but finally gains a new life (aided by Alidoro and Dandini, the Prince's tutor and valet) with an adoring prince (Ramiro). However, Rossini insisted that Ferretti purge the text of its supernatural elements: consequently, Angelina's good fortune is just that, with neither fairies nor spells to intervene. Ferretti also dispensed with the glass slipper, giving the lovers matching bracelets, and added to the happy ending Angelina's noble forgiveness of her ghastly family.

In outline, *La Cenerentola* looks like a conventional comic opera, but there are shades of darkness in this piece. Dandini is a gleeful manipulator, while Don Magnifico is a thoroughly loathsome specimen – witness his announcement to Alidoro that the "third sister" is dead, a piece of nastiness accompanied by minor-key tonalities and brittle orchestrations that reveal Cinderella's disbelief at his callousness. The lovers are the most substantial characters, especially Cinderella, whose personality develops as the opera proceeds. When, for example, the naive and bashful girl makes her first appearance in Act I, she is singing an inconsequential little tune that is very much in the comic tradition; but when she emerges at the ball she stands tall and proud, delivering powerfully florid music that transforms her into a romantic heroine. For much of the work Ramiro is a routine lyric tenor, but he leaps into a rather more heroic dimension whenever the moment demands – his Act II showstopper "Si, ritrovarla, io giuro" (Yes, I swear to find her) is a perfect example, with its ricochet intervals and barnstorming high Cs. This duality of *La Cenerentola*, its oscillations between pantomime and something altogether more ardent or serious, goes a long way to refuting the cliché that Rossini was, to quote the critic Cecil Gray, "a master of shallow waters" and nothing more.

Abbado's excellent recording followed a production at the 1970 Edinburgh Festival, and although it was taped in the studio it has all the sparkle and immediacy of a live event. This is in no small part thanks to Teresa Berganza. At 36 she was a little full-voiced for the young Cinderella, but her technical sureness, elegance and expressive range – the product of a decade of experience – are entrancing, and she makes a sensitive and determined heroine. Luigi Alva's tenor is nicely placed for Ramiro, with a gentle tone, elegant phrasing and an impressive line in high notes. The other cast members are excellent and LSO provide crisp, responsive support.

71

Gioacchino Rossini

Le Comte Ory

Juan Oncina (Count Ory), Sari Barabas (Adèle), Monica Sinclair (Ragonde), Michel Roux (Raimbaud); Glyndebourne Festival Chorus and Orchestra; Vittorio Gui (conductor)

EMI CMS7 64180-2; 2 CDs; mid-price

Le Comte Ory is arguably the finest of Rossini's many comedies. A real-life villain, Count Ory first appeared in fiction in an eighteenth-century ballad, which was turned into a one-act play by Scribe and Delestre-Poirson in 1817. They offered the yarn to Rossini, who requested a prefatory act to make the libretto long enough for a full evening's opera. Provided with his text, Rossini set about one of the greatest acts of self-theft in operatic history, making up half of *Ory's* score from *Il Viaggio a Rheims*, an opera he had written three years before. Parisian audiences were used to such practices, but Rossini's stunt was too much for his librettists, who were so ashamed of what they had helped perpetrate that neither would allow his name to be printed on the libretto.

They shouldn't have been so precious, for Rossini's treatment of the text was a fitting swan-song to his career as a composer of comic opera. Set to music of irresistible verve and fluency, the drama abounds with manic situations. Countess Adèle, Ragonde and their companions have taken a vow of chastity while their menfolk are on a Crusade in the Holy Land. The amorous Count Ory, aided and abetted by his tutor, his page Isolier and his friend Raimbaud, lays siege to the Countess, disguising himself first as a curer of lovesickness and secondly as a journeying nun. The "nuns" (Ory, Isolier and Raimbaud) get uproariously drunk and escape only just in time as the crusading menfolk return.

Le Comte Ory is dominated throughout by its title role, scored by Rossini for the highest of tenor voices: he sets the pace from his opening cavatina, "Que les destins prospères" (What a future awaits us), a delightfully unctuous prelude in which he offers his services to anyone who might be looking for a husband. Ory is allocated most of the finest music, and Rossini was clearly very fond of the character (Ory's duet with Isolier later in the same act has a vigour and good-natured charm that makes it difficult to deplore his chicanery), but – as with most of Rossini's comedies – the success of the opera really hangs on its superb ensembles, which invariably begin slowly and low on the stave and build into a crescendo of barely singable lunacy. *Ory's* finest ensemble, and the high spot of the entire work, occurs when Ory's "nuns" inveigle their way into the castle's wine cellars. Left to themselves, and dressed in full habits, they launch into a bawdy drinking song; when Adèle and Ragonde are heard approaching, however, they quickly turn the singalong into a sanctimonious prayer. The final trio between Ory, Adèle and Isolier is another sublime achievement, a Mozartian gem in which, despite the flurry of activity, each of the three is perfectly characterized through their melody. In the opinion of Hector Berlioz, it was Rossini's "absolute masterpiece".

Recorded in 1956, this performance of Ory did a lot to restore Rossini's reputation outside Italy, for Gui's conducting is frothy and spontaneous, and his cast is almost perfect. Juan Oncina's tenor was among the most versatile of the time, and this recording shows why he was celebrated for his performances of Rossini's lusty Count. Sari Barabas and Monica Sinclair are superb as Adèle and Ragonde, while Michel Roux is in his element as the clowning Raimbaud. The "nun" scenes are hilarious and beautifully timed, and this remains among the most wonderful recordings ever made of a Rossini opera, despite the mono sound and the excision of about fifteen minutes' worth of music.

72

Camille Saint-Saëns

Samson et Dalila

José Cura (Samson), Olga Borodina (Dalila), Jean-Philippe Lafont (Le Grand-Prêtre de Dagon), Egile Silins (Abimélech); London Symphony Orchestra and Chorus; Colin Davis (conductor)

Erato 3984-24756-2; 2 CDs; full price

Samson et Dalila is the only one of Saint-Saëns's thirteen operas that has achieved any lasting success. This fact was acutely regretted by the composer, who believed his operatic music to be among his best, but there's a straightforward explanation for it: *Samson* was the only one of Saint-Saëns' operas with any theatrical flair. Haunted by the ghost of Mozart, his operas embody many of the traditional qualities of French music – neatness, clarity and elegance – but formal precision tends to take precedence over characterization and dramatic impact. *Samson et Dalila* is the exception to the rule, and Liszt was so impressed that in 1870 he agreed to produce it in Weimar if Saint-Saëns ever completed it. Amazingly, he kept his word nearly eight years later, but the French premiere didn't come until 1890, for despite Saint-Saëns' reputation, the Paris Opéra refused to stage a work based upon the Bible.

Deeply impressed by the English oratorio tradition, and in particular by Mendelssohn's *Elijah*, Saint-Saëns originally intended to use the story of Samson for an oratorio. However, the poet and dramatist Ferdinand Lemaire saw theatrical potential in the story and convinced Saint-Saëns to turn it into an opera. The plot is as narrated in the Book of Judges: the Hebrew warrior Samson is seduced by the Philistine beauty Delilah; having discovered the secret of his great strength she betrays him to the Philistines; blinded and tied up in the temple, Samson is mocked and taunted, but when he prays to God his strength returns and he brings down the temple.

Although *Samson* has the trappings of Grand Opéra – ballets, big choruses, lengthy ensembles and a fair amount of spectacle – it is otherwise typical of the composer's cerebral approach to opera. At times the piece seems more suited to a church, and Saint-Saëns' taste for allusions to other composers (Bach for the Hebrews, Handel for the Philistines, a passing reference to Gounod as the satrap is killed) often suggest a man too pleased with his own cleverness. That said, much of Act III is sensationally dramatic, opening with Samson's melancholic treadmill aria "Vois ma misère, hélas" (See my misery, alas) before plunging into the barnstorming barbarism of the bacchanal – Saint-Saëns's most impressive orchestral showpiece.

Some French critics attacked what they perceived as the tunelessness of *Samson*, a perverse complaint, for Samson's ardent tenor and Dalila's rich mezzo-soprano carry some of the most beautiful vocal melodies in French opera – music that was later to become central to the repertoire of Parisian organ-grinders. Dalila's great Act II seduction aria "Mon cœur s'ouvre à toi" (My heart opens to you) is rightly the best-known music, but her Act I "Printemps qui commence" (Spring that comes) and her vibrant, sensual call to love at the beginning of Act II, "Amour! Viens aider ma faiblesse" (Love, help me in my weakness), are no less fine. For moments such as these it is easy to forgive Saint-Saëns his somewhat calculated manner.

Colin Davis's 1997 *Samson* is one of his finest opera recordings. Although made with a British orchestra and chorus, an Argentinian Samson and a Russian Dalila, this is a thoroughly integrated performance that throbs with tension. It stars two of today's most promising operatic talents: José Cura's tenor is the real thing, with grace as well as power, and the mezzo Olga Borodina makes a strikingly seductive Dalila. The supporting cast are all encouraged to ham it up to splendid effect, and Davis keeps his foot to the floor throughout – thrillingly so during the bacchanal.

73

Arnold Schoenberg

Erwartung

Jessye Norman (Woman); New York Metropolitan Orchestra; James Levine (conductor)

Philips 426 261-5PH; 1 CD; with cabaret songs; full price

In 1909, the year that *Erwartung* was composed, Schoenberg wrote what might be the single most influential piece of twentieth-century music – the *Three Pieces for Piano*, Opus 11. In these three epigrammatic works he made a break with the traditional vocabulary of Western music (key signatures, tonal centres, etc), inaugurating an atonal style in which all the notes of the chromatic scale were assigned equal importance. *Erwartung*, one of the masterworks of this revolutionary aesthetic, offers an intense and harrowing experience that is like no other opera. Indeed, some would say that it is not an opera at all: it lasts a little over thirty minutes, works almost as well in a concert hall as on stage, and has but a single protagonist, whose psychological traumas are externalized by the music. However, Schoenberg intended *Erwartung* to be staged, and even if it doesn't meet the standard criteria of opera, there isn't any other genre to which it more comfortably belongs.

Marie Pappenheim, the librettist of *Erwartung*, was a medical student as well as a poet, and her dramatized monologue has many of the qualities of a Freudian case history. The listener has no way of measuring the veracity of what is being said since the work's solitary character (referred to only as the Woman) inter-acts with no-one. The only thing that is clear is the sense of the Woman's psychological dislocation and instability, caused by the loss (real or imagined) of the object of her love. The story emerges through fragments of information: a nameless Woman walks through a moonlit forest (itself metaphorical of her mind) in search of her lover, encountering various reflections of her fearful and expectant state of mind. Eventually she discovers the body of her lover. Lying down beside him, she accuses him of infidelity and wonders what to do with her life; in the end she rises to her feet and leaves.

Pappenheim's text was in part influenced by a crisis in Schoenberg's household: his wife had recently ended a passionate affair with the painter Richard Gerstl, who had then killed himself. Schoenberg completed the score in just over two weeks, but the intensity and rawness of the finished product delayed its premiere until 1924, fifteen years later. He matched Pappenheim's language with the most improvisatory and expressionistic music he ever wrote, setting the words to a mild form of *Sprechgesang* or "speech-song", a style of expressive vocal declamation mid-way between speech and singing, in which the voice briefly touches the indicated pitch without sustaining it. The rapidity of the mood swings – with moments of apparent lucidity next to episodes of near-incoherence – are brilliantly communicated through the music's rhythmic freedom, while the absence of a clear pulse, like the absence of tonality, contributes to a sensation of rootlessness and timelessness – as if the entire work were unfolding inside the woman's head. The orchestra is large but the instruments are used in richly varied chamber-like combinations, creating an atmospheric commentary on what is happening.

Erwartung works well on record, and there is no better recording than James Levine's 1993 account, with Jessye Norman as the Woman. She uses her massive voice with remarkable delicacy, bringing uncommon beauty to the nightmarish portrayal. Levine succeeds not only in producing a luscious sound from the Met Orchestra, but also in highlighting the overall structure of the score. This is demanding music, but it's sung and played so dramatically that it makes an ideal introduction to the composer's more difficult work. It's accompanied by remarkably witty performances of Schoenberg's *Cabaret Songs*.

74

Arnold Schoenberg

Moses und Aron

David Pittman-Jennings (Moses), Chris Merritt (Aron), László Polgár (Priest),
Gabriele Fontana (Young Girl), Yvonne Naef (Invalid Woman); Netherlands
Opera Chorus; Concertgebouw Orchestra; Pierre Boulez (conductor)

Deutsche Grammophon 449 174-2GH2; 2 CDs; full price

An unresolved need for communication with God was central to
Schoenberg's personality, and for
most of his life he was racked by
the problems of self-knowledge
and religious belief. His regular
conversions to and abandonment
of Judaism were indicative of the
anguish he suffered, and in *Moses
und Aron* he wrestled with the
issue of humanity's inability to deal with absolute truth – as
given to Moses by God. The work was left incomplete at his
death, not because of shortage of time, but because Schoenberg
found it impossible to create music for the final act, in which
Moses berates Aaron for his devotion to the Image rather than to
the Idea. Schoenberg wrote in 1950 that he "agreed the third act
may simply be spoken, in case I cannot complete the composition" but the first staged performance omitted the act completely, which is now standard practice.

Schoenberg's narrative develops episodes from the Book of
Exodus, beginning with God's instruction to Moses to lead the
Israelites to the Promised Land. After much deprivation, the
Israelites begin to turn against Moses; his brother Aaron then
leads a group in the building of a golden calf. His brother returns
with the tablets to find his people in chaos; he destroys the image
and places Aaron in chains. Later, Aaron is freed, but as his
chains fall to the ground, he dies.

Even incomplete, this is still Schoenberg's grandest stage work and the most complete dramatic expression of his serialist techniques. The twelve-tone system, even when used with the flexibility that Schoenberg gives to it, brings problems – primarily in the delineation of character, because the tone-row makes it difficult to construct distinct sound-prints for each protagonist. But Schoenberg generates a dramatic charge by writing the baritone role of Moses in *Sprechgesang* while creating Aron's part as a fully scored role for a very high tenor, as far from the style of Moses as could be imagined. As a result an almost delirious intensity is generated in the clashes between Moses, the believer in God as "pure thought", and Aaron, who doubts that anyone loves what "they dare not imagine". But although the drama hinges on their relationship, the musical interest is dominated by the huge chorus, part of which is used (in the form of six voices) to represent the voice of God. Indeed, there are few operas more dependent upon the skill of its chorus. Only in the Stravinskian "Dance around the Golden Calf" – where Schoenberg relieves the tension of the tone-row with music of sumptuous colour – does the orchestra dominate the proceedings. Otherwise, as with *Erwartung*, Schoenberg uses his orchestral forces with great economy, brilliantly controlling the contrasts of scale between the symphonic and the chamber-like. For all the difficulty of the music, the emotional power of *Moses und Aron* is as direct as anything by any of Schoenberg's more traditional contemporaries.

The most recent recording – Boulez's second, dating from 1995 – is the finer. The most remarkable of the universally excellent performances is Chris Merritt's Aaron. Famed for his performances of high bel canto roles, Merritt was an inspired choice for the infamously punishing tenor role and, like no other, he manages to get around the music while, at the same time, conveying something of the character's tortured progress. David Pittman-Jennings' Moses is a suitably commanding presence, and the chorus of the Netherlands Opera cope brilliantly with the difficult part work. Boulez is in electrifying form, and the Concertgebouw bring warmth and cohesion, as well as excitement, to Schoenberg's score.

75

Bedřich Smetana

The Bartered Bride

Gabriela Beňačková (Mařenka), Petr Dvorský (Vašek), Richard Novák (Kecal), Miroslav Kopp (Jeník); Czech Philharmonic Chorus and Orchestra; Zdeněk Košler (conductor)

Supraphon 103511-2; 3 CDs; full price

Although Prague was one of the great musical centres of the eighteenth century, the Czech lands didn't start producing home-grown operas until the middle of the nineteenth century, when Bedřich Smetana came along. Smetana's style was strongly indebted to Italian opera and to Wagner, but his absorption of his country's folk songs marks him as the first Czech to bring his nation's musical culture to Europe-wide attention. His most successful work, and the most enduringly popular Eastern European opera, is *The Bartered Bride*, a sparkling rustic comedy that transcends the work's cultural boundaries. Its success was by no means immediate, however. The first version – premiered in 1866 – was in two long acts and suffered from some heavy-going spoken dialogue; when this failed, Smetana revised the score, cut the second act into two and replaced the dialogue with recitative. The new opera was an enormous hit, and by 1927 it had been performed a thousand times in Prague alone.

Much of *The Bartered Bride's* charm rests with Karel Sabina's libretto, and the immediacy of the characters Mařenka, Vašek and Kecal. The plot is simplicity itself. The peasant girl Mařenka loves handsome but poor Jeník, but her parents engage the scheming marriage broker Kecal to find her a rich husband. He introduces them to Vašek, the simple son of Tobias Mícha. The furious

Mařenka tracks Vašek down and discourages him from marriage. Meanwhile, Kecal offers Jeník a bribe if he will let Mařenka go. He agrees – on condition that she marries "the eldest son of Tobias Mícha". After many misunderstandings, it emerges that Jeník is the eldest son: not only does he secure Mařenka's hand in marriage, he also gets to keep Kecal's generous bribe.

As with most of Smetana's music, *The Bartered Bride* is built from simple basic material, which is then often developed in a sophisticated manner. A fine example of this is the Act I love duet between Mařenka and Jeník: like all this opera's vocal melodies it is made up of ideas taken from Czech folk song, but Smetana enhances the intensity of the moment through the use of a flowing orchestral undercurrent and rich harmonic patterns, turning the duet's central theme into a "love" motif that runs through the whole opera. Smetana's technical expertise is never obtrusive or complicated – not a single line of the opera is beyond the efforts of a good amateur singer, which is how it had to be, given the resources of the young Provincial Theatre. And though there are elements of Italian fluency and German declamation in Smetana's style, the metre and the pulse of the vocal parts are dictated by the character of the Czech language. The stuttering, lovelorn Vašek, the bossy mother, the earnest but canny lovers and the cheerfully scheming Kecal are empathetic characters with authentic-sounding voices, and it is this sense of authenticity – along with the opera's bold contrasts of mood and atmosphere (thought by Smetana to be a "Czech quality") – that propelled *The Bartered Bride* to international popularity.

Zdeněk Košler's 1980 recording was made to accompany a film of the opera, which is also available on video. He is an eager, imaginative conductor and he generates some exquisite playing from the Czech Philharmonic. The casting is dominated by the sweet tenor voices of Petr Dvorský and Miroslav Kopp as Jeník and Vašek. Gabriela Beňačková is in no less beautiful voice as Mařenka, and the "character" bass Richard Novák is outrageously over the top as the doddery Kecal. Everyone sounds like they are enjoying themselves, and the fresh digital sound completes the attraction of this outstanding performance.

76

Johann Strauss the Younger

Die Fledermaus

Julia Varady (Rosalinde), Lucia Popp (Adele), Hermann Prey (Eisenstein), René Kollo (Alfred), Bernd Weikl (Falke), Ivan Rebroff (Orlovsky); Bavarian State Opera Chorus and Orchestra; Carlos Kleiber (conductor)

Deutsche Grammophon DG 415 646-2; 2 CDs; full price

Just as Offenbach's operettas embodied the spirit of the French Second Empire at its most corpulent, so Johann Strauss the Younger's music epitomized the riotous decadence of the Austro-Hungarian Empire – nowhere more so than in *Die Fledermaus* (The Bat), an opera in which luscious music disguises a mordant critique of the audience at which it's aimed. The management of the Theater an der Wien found it too close to the knuckle, and even after editing it caused something of a scandal, while others had problems with the unintelligible plot. Within two years, however, it was being performed throughout Europe and America and, in 1890 the Vienna Opera took the extraordinary step of adding this operetta to its repertoire.

The plot underwent many changes before Strauss finally committed himself to setting it to music, and considering the complexity of the final version you can only wonder what the first draft must have been like. In essence, a group of friends and rivals (Eisenstein, his wife Rosalinde, Alfred the opera singer, Doctor Falke, Adele and Frank) attend a party at Prince Orlofsky's where each is caught in the act of seducing someone else's partner. The opera ends in praise of champagne, on which the evening's numerous indiscretions are blamed.

Gingered up with bits of quasi-Hungarian local colour, the score has all the sparkle you'd expect from the creator of the "Blue

Danube" waltz, and Strauss demonstrates a brilliant handling of structure and pacing, as well as a flair for character-drawing: each of the cast has reason for behaving as he or she does, which is not the case with most operettas. Whereas Offenbach's caricatures were often targeted at real-life individuals, Strauss's satire is more generic, but no less acute: Orlofsky is an unforgettable image of aristocratic degeneracy, adroitly cast by Strauss as a mezzo in drag, a device that gives the character an overtone of slippery sexuality. Moreover, Strauss couches his satire in a more "cultured" musical language than that of Offenbach. Indeed, *Die Fledermaus* is the most operatic of operettas. The orchestra here plays a far more prominent role than in most operettas, presenting principal themes and defining character rather than merely serving as accompaniment. Similarly, the vocal score is decidedly grown-up: only the comic role of Frosch can be played by an untrained voice, and only the very greatest singers can hope to tackle Adele or Rosalinde, whose Hungarian-style aria in Act II is an absolute blinder.

Strauss's analysis of his society is cynical, but the way he presents it is full of vivacity. No matter what deception or dishonesty is occurring, the music is all about fun and escapism, as exemplified by such highlights as Adele's laughing aria "Mein Herr Marquis", Orlofsky's toast to champagne, and Falke's hymn to love, "Brüderlein und Schwesterlein" (Little brother and sister). Constructed with a classical precision that Mozart might have approved, *Die Fledermaus* is, in short, something of a Trojan Horse.

With this 1976 recording Carlos Kleiber in effect reinvented a score that had come to sound hackneyed in most hands. The wit, elegance and vitality of his conducting are a constant revelation, inspiring his cast to perhaps the finest ensemble performance of the opera on CD. Julia Varady is glorious as Rosalinde, Lucia Popp makes an exacting Adele, René Kollo is a spirited Alfred and Hermann Prey is perfectly smooth as Eisenstein. The characterizations are nicely defined throughout, and Prey's big duet with Bernd Weikl's Falke is tremendous fun. The sole weakness is the casting of coloratura bass Ivan Rebroff as a falsetto Orlofsky, but this is still a hugely rewarding experience.

Richard Strauss

Salome

Cheryl Studer (Salome), Bryn Terfel (Jokanaan), Horst Hiestermann (Herod), Leonie Rysanek (Herodias), Clemens Bieber (Narraboth); Berlin Deutsche Oper Orchestra; Giuseppe Sinopoli (conductor)

Deutsche Grammophon 431 810-2GH2; 2 CDs; full price

In 1904 Richard Strauss was Germany's most popular living composer; the following year, after the first performance of *Salome*, he became its most controversial. The choice of Oscar Wilde's notorious play as the source for his opera was in itself something of a gesture of affiliation with the avant-garde, and throughout the project's two-year gestation rumours abounded about the radicalism of Strauss's venture. But few anticipated the daring of the single-span, eighty-minute score, which perfectly fitted the violence and febrile eroticism of Wilde's symbolist tragedy.

Strauss worked on the libretto himself and, through careful editing, concentrated attention on the relationship between Salome and Jokanaan (John the Baptist). Set in King Herod's palace, the action is limited to a handful of scenes with an unchanging set. Salome is fascinated by the holy man locked in the castle dungeon but she cannot understand how he can resist her charms. She vows that they will kiss, whether he likes it or not. Herod is terrified by Jokanaan's curses and fears his predictions of the arrival of "one greater" than himself. By way of distraction Herod implores Salome to dance (the "Dance of the Seven Veils") – in return for which she demands the head of Jokanaan on a platter. Herod reluctantly agrees, but when he sees her kissing the severed head of the Baptist he orders his soldiers to crush her to death.

There are many *fin de siècle* themes running beneath *Salome's* blood-red surface, notably the Freudian dynamic by which the sexually abused Salome, who has been violated by her stepfather, becomes the abuser of Narraboth and Jokanaan, both of whom die through their contact with her. Some nasty ideas about race and religion are embodied by Salome's degeneration (a consequence of her exposure to Jewry) and the characterization of the "Five Jews" and Herod as emasculated trouble-makers. Many, however, find *Salome* an hypnotic and erotically charged experience, despite the tawdriness of its underlying concepts.

The prevalence of minor keys (only Jokanaan gets major-key music) and constantly changing textures maintains a sense of tension and unease which is released only at the end, when Salome kisses the Baptist to some of the most gloriously indulgent music ever written. Strauss's unsettling manner of setting lyrical vocal melodies over an outlandishly contrapuntal foundation is typified by the confrontation between Salome and Herod when, the Princess having removed her final veil, the King's delight turns to horror upon realizing that Salome will take nothing but the Baptist's head as her reward. With each succeeding offer, his tenor rises higher and the orchestra becomes ever more fraught until, exhausted, he concedes despairingly to his stepdaughter's gruesome demand. Strauss wanted Salome to be sung by "a sixteen-year-old Isolde" and it is certainly one of the most taxing of all roles, demanding an equal measure of delicacy and power. Salome's vocalizing oscillates between bestial ferocity and child-like compassion and culminates in a glowing stream of sound – the chilling declaration of love that precedes her death.

Giuseppe Sinopoli's 1990 recording of *Salome* is the finest of recent years, thanks chiefly to the casting of Cheryl Studer as Salome. Hers is a light soprano, with a quivering quality that's ideal for the portrayal of Strauss's unstable heroine, and she brilliantly captures the role's fragility, youth and burgeoning sexuality. Bryn Terfel's Jokanaan is sumptuous, and Horst Hiestermann and Leonie Rysanek are memorably vile as the Herods. Sinopoli directs a marvellously fluid performance, demonstrating remarkable restraint and a superb ear for musical colour and shape.

Richard Strauss

Elektra

Inge Borkh (Elektra), Marianne Schech (Chrysothemis), Jean Madeira
(Clytemnestra), Dietrich Fischer-Dieskau (Orestes), Fritz Uhl (Aegisthus);
Dresden Staatskapelle Opera Chorus and Orchestra; Karl Böhm (conductor)

Deutsche Grammophon 445 329-2GX2; 2 CDs; mid-price

In 1903 Max Reinhardt followed his long-running production of Wilde's *Salome* with a reworking of Sophocles' *Elektra* by Hugo von Hofmannsthal. Strauss saw the production two years later and was struck by the musical potentialities of the play, which pushed the ancient tragedy to dysfunctional extremes. However, he was worried by the similarities he saw between Hofmannsthal's work and his own recent setting of the Salome story. Hofmannsthal reassured him: "The blend of colour in the two subjects strikes me as quite different in all essentials; in *Salome* much is, so to speak, purple and violet, and the atmosphere is torrid. In *Elektra*, on the other hand, it is a mixture of might and light, or black and bright." Hofmannsthal raised Strauss's game, spurring the composer to produce what is his finest stage work, and one of the greatest music-dramas ever written.

The opera begins with Elektra mourning the murder of her father Agamemnon by her mother Clytemnestra, against whom she vows revenge. Her sister Chrysothemis has chosen to stay with her mother, but Elektra lives outside the city "like a dog", howling abuse and condemnation at Clytemnestra and her new husband Aegisthus. Her brother Orestes returns and slays Clytemnestra, Aegisthus and most of their supporters. Delirious with joy, Elektra sings a duet with her sister, and dances herself to death.

As Hofmannsthal later admitted, his *Elektra* cried out for musical treatment, and Strauss threw everything into the colossal ninety-minute score. On one level it contains all the pictorialism associated with his orchestral music (barking dogs, jangling jewellery, etc), but on a much deeper level it portrays the psychological extremism of the characters to perfection. The revolting Clytemnestra, for example, is portrayed through music of near atonal dissonance, while Chrysothemis is all major keys and ardent lyricism. The axis of the opera is Elektra herself, who is on stage for most of the time, and is required to sing nearly an hour of music that ranges between shrieking hysteria, loving tenderness (famously during the scene in which she is greeted by Orestes) and, come the conclusion, self-destructive jubilation. While little of what precedes the final duet with her sister might be considered traditionally beautiful, the final ten minutes are the very incarnation of ecstasy, and among the most exciting music you will ever hear. In the immediacy of Elektra's hatred for her mother, her love for Orestes and her disgust with her sister Chrysothemis, Strauss was inspired to levels of inventiveness that he was never to equal. Orestes is a less substantial creation, but he is the only source of light or hope in the work, and the "Recognition Scene" between brother and sister – the one unequivocally major-key episode – is the poignant climax of the opera, the point at which the drama finally turns to Elektra's advantage.

One of the century's greatest opera recordings, this 1960 Deutsche Grammophon production captured Inge Borkh in her prime. Her soprano is not especially big, but it is dramatically projected and her variety of tone enables the character to develop as the events overtake her – the woman who sings the opening monologue is not the same as the one singing herself to death in the final scene. Jean Madeira is Clytemnestra, and no singer has ever conveyed so convincing an impression of disintegrating sanity, and all with the most amazing technical assurance. In support, Fischer-Dieskau makes a powerful Orestes and Marianne Schech is an intense Chrysothemis. Controlling all this talent is Karl Böhm whose feel for the internal pulse of Strauss's score brings the opera throbbingly to life.

Richard Strauss

Der Rosenkavalier

Christa Ludwig (Marschallin), Tatiana Troyanos (Octavian), Edith Mathis (Sophie), Theo Adam (Baron Ochs); Vienna State Opera Chorus; Vienna Philharmonic Orchestra; Karl Böhm (conductor)

Deutsche Grammophon 445 338-2GX3; 3 CDs; mid-price

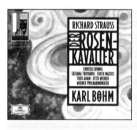

Der Rosenkavalier was conceived by Hofmannsthal as an eighteenth-century comedy of manners, in the style of Molière and the Mozart/Da Ponte operas – above all the *Marriage of Figaro*. But the vision of *Rosenkavalier* is nostalgic and romantic, with none of the subversive undercurrents of *Figaro*. Celebrating the *ancien régime* rather than criticizing it, *Rosenkavalier* has a delicate humour and charm that Strauss and his librettist were confident would bring success, and they were right – special "Rosenkavalier" trains were soon shuttling audiences to Dresden from all over Germany, and Strauss became a very rich man. Some find this piece too sweet and contrived, but many would concur with Debussy's verdict: "There is sunshine in the music of Strauss . . . it is not possible to withstand his irresistible domination."

Like *Figaro*, *Rosenkavalier* concerns the sexual antics of two couples – the Marschallin and her seventeen-year-old lover, Count Octavian (played by a soprano), and Sophie von Faninal and her boorish fiancé Baron Ochs. The Marschallin is some years older than Octavian and secretly yearns for him to marry Sophie, who is much better suited in age and temperament. But when, dressed as a serving girl, the fleeing Octavian is spotted by Ochs the situation becomes complicated. After much confusion and with Ochs humiliated, the Marschallin relinquishes Octavian to Sophie, and all ends happily.

Urged by Hofmannsthal to create a "Viennese comedy, not a Berlin farce", Strauss devised a delicious concoction laced with passionate vocal writing, most of it conceived in a surprisingly conversational manner. This relaxed, almost ingenuous quality disguises the opera's complexity – there are more subtly interconnected leitmotifs in *Der Rosenkavalier* than in any other of his operas – but for most people the structural ingenuity takes a distant second place to the beauty of the vocal score.

With the uproarious prelude over, *Der Rosenkavalier* is dominated by its melodies, most of which belong to the soprano roles of Octavian, Sophie and the Marschallin. On one level the work is a showcase for the soprano voice, and sopranos have queued up to display their mettle in such glorious episodes as the final scene of Act I, the Act II "Presentation of the Rose" and the famous final trio of Act III, in which Strauss entwines all three soprano leads in a seven-minute scene of intoxicating beauty. Of the male voices, Ochs is all aristocratic pomposity, and his music is suitably gruff and outsized, but Strauss's lyrical proclivities are given vent in such interludes as the Italian Tenor's aria (a Mozart pastiche sung by a nameless walk-on). For all the succulence of the voices, *Der Rosenkavalier* is also a celebration of the waltz, a form with which it anachronistically abounds. Derived from the music of Schubert, Lanner and Johann Strauss the Younger, the opera's waltzes are so refined and plausible that you might be tricked into thinking that they must have been a feature of eighteenth-century life.

Karl Böhm recorded *Rosenkavalier* in the studio in 1958, but that set pales beside this 1969 live recording from the Vienna Staatsoper. The beauty and warmth of Christa Ludwig's Marschallin, the urgency of Tatiana Troyanos's Octavian and the fragile innocence of Edith Mathis's Sophie have never been bettered. Theo Adam's Ochs is a complicated, intelligent creation, and Böhm's favourite tenor, Anton de Ridder, delivers the goods as the Italian Singer. Böhm's feel for the opera's overall shape, orchestral texture and phrasing is unequalled. From start to finish, this is the most consistently beautiful performance on record.

80

Igor Stravinsky

The Rake's Progress

Anthony Rolfe-Johnson (Tom Rakewell), Sylvia McNair (Anne Trulove), Paul Plishka (Nick Shadow); Tokyo Opera Singers; Saito Kinen Orchestra; Seiji Ozawa (conductor)

Philips 454 431–2; 2 CDs; full price

Stravinsky's remarkable career exemplifies the stylistic plurality of twentieth-century music. Just three years after making his name with the opulent, late-Romantic ballet *The Firebird* (1910), he created *The Rite of Spring*, a viscerally exciting piece that achieved instant notoriety. Soon after his music underwent another major change, as he adopted a cool, restrained and fastidious neo-classical language, a phase that culminated with *The Rake's Progress*, premiered in 1951.

Asked by Stravinsky to write a libretto based on Hogarth's paintings of the same name, W. H. Auden and Chester Kallman came up with a text that mixed in references to other Hogarth images and beefed up the scope of their morality tale with allusions to *Don Giovanni* and *Faust*. Stravinsky worked on the score, to the exclusion of all else, for three years, and his creative relationship with Auden – a fellow Christian – was extremely successful. Upon hearing the first performance in Venice, Dylan Thomas was moved to remark "Auden is the most skilful of us all", and the libretto of *The Rake's Progress* did indeed give Stravinsky the perfect vehicle for his virtuosity. A savagely ironic opera, it concerns the vanity and greed of Tom Rakewell who, rather than work, sells his soul to Nick Shadow, in the process losing the love of his life, Anne Trulove, and ending up mad in an asylum. (The opera's epilogue and moral is "For idle hands,

And hearts and minds, The Devil finds a work to do.") It might not sound like it, but *The Rake's Progress* is outrageously funny, and stands as one of the wittiest operas ever created.

Stravinsky matched his music to Hogarth's eighteenth-century milieu, constructing a sound-world that can best be described as a respectful parody of the Baroque. Constructed from solo and ensemble numbers accompanied by a small, beautifully scored chamber orchestra and strung together by recitatives accompanied by harpsichord, this opera constantly invokes Mozart, Haydn, Pergolesi and John Gay's *Beggar's Opera* (see p.53). In addition, there are allusions to Monteverdi in the mix (the action commences with a fanfare that invokes the opening of *Orfeo*), and Stravinsky also pays homage to nineteenth-century bel canto style in some of the arias, notably in some exquisite, languid melodies for Anne, most famously "Gently, little boat, across the water float". Yet throughout *The Rake's Progress* there's a distinctively modern and Stravinskian feel to the often odd metrical emphasis and angular harmonies, so that one is constantly aware that the music of the eighteenth century is being placed, as it were, in inverted commas. With its subtle anachronisms, the music mirrors a world in which the natural order – epitomized by marriage, the family and country life – is subverted by Tom's fecklessness, and in its extremely knowing exploitation of opera's heritage, *The Rake's Progress* marks the apotheosis of Stravinsky's neo-classical style.

There have been many recordings of *The Rake's Progress*, including one of the first performance, conducted by the composer, but the finest is the most recent, taped from live performances conducted by Seiji Ozawa in 1995. Ozawa brings a refreshing seriousness to the score, particularly during the debt collection scene between Nick and Tom in Act III, but he is also more than usually sensitive to the lyricism of Stravinsky's writing – a quality frequently lost beneath the spiky rhythms and punchy counterpoint. Sylvia McNair is glorious as Anne and the veteran tenor Anthony Rolfe-Johnson brings rare weight to the tragic Tom. Paul Plishka's Shadow is excellently judged, as are the performances of Donald Adams (Trulove), Jane Henschel (Baba the Turk) and Ian Bostridge (Sellem).

81

Arthur Sullivan

The Mikado

Donald Adams (The Mikado), Anthony Rolfe-Johnson (Nanki-Poo), Richard Suart (Ko-Ko), Richard Van Allan (Pooh-Bah), Marie McLaughlin (Yum-Yum); Welsh National Opera Orchestra and Chorus; Charles Mackerras (conductor)

Telarc CD80284; 1 CD; full price

Arthur Sullivan was England's most significant native composer since the death of Purcell, a century and a half before Sullivan's birth. While he failed to revitalize England's musical reputation abroad, his witty burlesques were as typically English as Offenbach's were French and Strauss's were Austrian. Most of his stage works were the product of his celebrated collaboration with the playwright and satirist William Gilbert, a relationship famously nurtured by the impresario Richard D'Oyly Carte, who established London's Savoy Theatre purely as a showcase for their works. *The Mikado*, which ran for 627 consecutive performances, was the biggest of their Savoy hits.

In October 1884 Sullivan informed D'Oyly Carte that he would compose nothing more for the Savoy: "My tunes are in danger of becoming mere repetitions of my former pieces," he wrote. But just a few weeks later he was toying with the idea of writing an operetta that would appeal to the vogue for "something Japanese". Both Gilbert and Sullivan had attended a Japanese exhibition in London, which had led to friendships with a number of Japanese expatriates, whose reports of life back home helped G & S in their creation of Titipu, setting of *The Mikado*. The plot concerns the troubadour Nanki-Poo, the son of the Mikado (Emperor), and his efforts to marry Yum-Yum, who is engaged to marry her guardian Ko-Ko, the Lord High Executioner – convoluted process that involves a variety of absurd characters, including Pitti-Sing, Peep-Bo and Pooh-Bah ("Lord High Everything Else"). Titipu is essentially England in oriental clothing, and most of its absurdities were parodies of English custom and pretension – just as the musical fabric, for all its oriental overtones, owes most to English music. Pooh-Bah, in particular, is an uproarious embodiment of corruption and the evils of privilege, revelling in his ability to trace his "ancestry back to a protoplasmal primordial atomic globule".

Gilbert's text was well judged to serve his partner, providing templates for a huge variety of musical forms and numbers, including some inspired jokes – such as Katisha's "Oh faithless one, this insult you shall rue", in which she attempts to reveal Nanki-Poo's identity only to be drowned out at every turn by the chorus. Gilbert created lines that invited Sullivan to indulge his love of musical parody, notably of Bach, Handel and Beethoven, though there are allusions to at least half a dozen of his more serious contemporaries. Victorian ballads are nicely set against more acerbic pastiches, and many of the work's best numbers have lodged in the English collective unconscious: Ko-Ko's "Tit-willow" refrain, for example, will be recognized by many who think they don't know any Gilbert and Sullivan.

Charles Mackerras's reputation is now inextricably linked to the music of Dvořák and Janáček, but when he first arrived in England from Australia in the 1940s he made his reputation with a ballet – *Pineapple Poll* – based on themes from G & S's operettas. He has thankfully not abandoned this aspect of his conducting career, and at least half a dozen G & S recordings bear his name. This is the finest of his G & S series for Telarc, and certainly the best-sung *Mikado* on disc, with a world-class operatic cast letting their hair down. It's been trimmed savagely to fit onto a single CD – the dialogue omitted and the overture cut – but Mackerras is in sparkling form, and the performances are universally marvellous, with Richard Van Allan's Pooh-Bah and Anthony Rolfe-Johnson's Nanki-Poo especially lovable. Marie McLaughlin is at ease as Yum-Yum and Felicity Palmer has a whale of a time as Katisha.

82

Pyotr Il'yich Tchaikovsky

Eugene Onegin

Galina Vishnevskaya (Tatyana), Yevgeny Belov (Onegin), Sergei Lemeshev (Lensky): Bolshoi Theatre Chorus and Orchestra; Boris Khaikin (conductor)

Melodiya 74321 17090-2; 2 CDs; mid-price

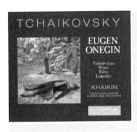

All of Tchaikovsky's music was first and foremost conceived for the voice – whether or not it was actually written for the voice, his music can always be sung. There's an irony, then, in the fact that he's now best known for his symphonies, concertos and ballets, for Tchaikovsky's operas are the distillation of what he termed his "lyrical idea", the notion that everything can be characterized or embodied through melody. He had already written four operas by the time he came to compose *Eugene Onegin*, a project he commenced after being greatly impressed by performances of *Carmen* and the *Ring* cycle. A more personal inspiration was the letter he received in May 1877 from a besotted female pupil, Antonina Milyukova, who was still unaware of the composer's homosexuality. Later that month a friend suggested to Tchaikovsky that he turn Pushkin's great verse-novel *Eugene Onegin* into an opera. Coming to the passage where the heroine reveals her love for Onegin in a letter, Tchaikovsky began to set the scene to music. He completed *Onegin* at the end of 1879, by which time he and Milyukova had married and separated.

In Pushkin's poem the young and romantically disposed Tatyana falls in love with Onegin, whose friend Lensky is smitten by Tatyana's sister Olga. Tatyana pours out her heart in a letter to Onegin, which he rejects, proposing they see no more of each other. Onegin and Lensky attend Tatyana's birthday party, during which Onegin flirts with Olga – who responds positively to his flirtation. Lensky challenges his friend to a duel, in which he is killed. Six years later Onegin returns to find Tatyana married to Prince Gremin. Realizing he loved her after all, he begs her to elope. She refuses, though she still loves him, and he leaves.

Characterized by Tchaikovsky as "lyrical scenes in three acts and seven tableaux", *Onegin* is concerned more with character and emotional timbre than with linear narrative, as it charts Tatyana's transformation from a girl into a woman and Onegin's from a "gentleman" into a man. Initially Tatyana is established through music of rustic charm and simplicity – open-hearted, rhythmically upbeat, melodically fluid and generally major key. Her letter scene is Italianate in its warmth and eloquence, but for the climactic confrontation in the third act her music has become reined-in and bitter. With Onegin the process is reversed: in Act I his patronizing sophistication is defined by stark minor-key phrases, and it is not until Onegin acknowledges his love for Tatyana in the final act that Tchaikovsky opens out his music to reflect the feelings of this "boy in spellbound passion". Lensky and Olga are little more than foils to the central relationship, but for the scene preceding his duel with Onegin Tchaikovsky gave Lensky one of the greatest tenor arias in Russian music, "Faint echo of my heart" – a pain-filled song that is probably the opera's best-known music.

This melancholy scene is sung on Boris Khaikin's superb recording of *Eugene Onegin* by the legendary lyric tenor Sergei Lemeshev, but the performance is dominated by Galina Vishnevskaya's Tatyana. Her range of expression is simply bewildering, and more than any other soprano she presents a graphic transformation from girlish coyness to womanly confidence. Yevgeny Belov has a fine baritone, and his portrayal of Onegin is no less comprehensive. Boris Khaikin demonstrates an infallible feel for the score's nuances of mood and texture, and the Russian orchestra and chorus give their all. The sound is mono, but of excellent quality for 1955.

83

Pyotr Il'yich Tchaikovsky

The Queen of Spades

Vladimir Atlantov (Hermann), Mirella Freni (Lisa), Maureen Forrester (Countess), Sergei Leiferkus (Tomsky), Dmitri Hvorostovsky (Yeletsky); Tanglewood Festival Chorus; Boston Symphony Orchestra; Seiji Ozawa (conductor)

RCA 09026 60992; 3 CDs; full price

Tchaikovsky followed *Eugene Onegin* with another opera based on a Pushkin text – *The Queen of Spades* (also known by its French title, *Pique Dame*). The idea was proposed by the composer's brother, Modest, who also suggested that he should write the libretto himself. At the end of 1889, after a year's delay, Tchaikovsky agreed to the collaboration, with the proviso that Modest rewrite the ending in line with his requirements, the chief of which was that the two lead characters should kill themselves – a revision typical of a composer who, to quote one critic, was becoming increasingly occupied with "emotions bordering on hysteria".

The narrative is otherwise consistent with its source. An army officer, Hermann, loves Lisa, the granddaughter of the Countess – a famously successful gambler known as the Queen of Spades. Hermann becomes obsessed with the secret of the Countess's success, and breaks into her bedroom with a pistol to demand the answer, whereupon the Countess dies of fright. The ghost of the Countess returns to give Hermann her secret: "Three…seven…ace." Lisa still loves Hermann and begs him to meet her, but his feelings for Lisa are overtaken by his need to put her grandmother's secret to the test. When he fails to show up, Lisa drowns herself. At the card table, Hermann is tricked by the Countess, loses his mind and stabs himself.

The Queen of Spades is Tchaikovsky's most theatrical opera, and the characters are kept just short of boiling point as the hand of Fate guides them towards their doom (as in *Onegin*, this opera features a prominent "Fate" motif). This intensity is balanced, however, by a skilled evocation of the world of Mozart and the Rococo style of Catherine the Great's St Petersburg. For example, in Lisa's first scene she accompanies herself (on the harpsichord) in an old-fashioned duet with her companion Pauline; in the Act II Interlude (a masked ball) Tchaikovsky presents a touching pastiche of eighteenth-century opera ("The Faithful Shepherdess"), with music that might easily be mistaken for Mozart; and, at the end of the act, the Countess's death – the most disturbing scene in all of Tchaikovsky's operas – is preceded by her singing of an air by the eighteenth-century Belgian composer André Grétry. It could be said that the juxtaposition of high emotion and delicate, archaic music is the dramatic principle of *The Queen of Spades*.

The tenor role of Hermann inspired Tchaikovsky to write his most forceful and dramatic operatic music. Initially a dignified, if excitable, member of the officer class, he begins the opera singing the sort of sweet, sophisticated music you'd expect of a romantic lead, but by the time he comes to play his final hand he is a psychotic paranoiac, and his music has become shockingly high and declamatory, full of wild intervals that are both grotesque and thrilling. Lisa, on the other hand, is a rather tepid creature, totally overshadowed by the dark, low-lying mezzo role of the Countess.

Seiji Ozawa's 1992 recording is one of the finest of anything by Tchaikovsky. As the Countess, Maureen Forrester sounds the right sort of age (she was sixty at the time) and hers is a shocking portrayal of a cruel and domineering woman. Mirella Freni was too old to play Lisa on stage, but she sings beautifully throughout, rising magnificently to the challenge in her love duets with the astonishing tenor Vladimir Atlantov, who steals the show with his extraordinarily troubled account of Hermann. Ozawa keeps the action fluid and the contrasts precise, and the Boston orchestra, while over-polished, are clear and well balanced.

84

Michael Tippett

The Midsummer Marriage

Joan Carlyle (Jenifer), Elizabeth Harwood (Bella), Alberto Remedios (Mark), Stuart Burrows (Jack); Royal Opera House Chorus and Orchestra; Colin Davis (conductor)

Lyrita SRCD2217; 2 CDs; full price

Michael Tippett was one of the very few English composers to have established an international reputation as a composer of opera, but had it not been for the great success of his friend Benjamin Britten's *Peter Grimes* (see p.31) in 1945 Tippett might never have written for the stage. Although Tippett was the older composer (born 1905), he enjoyed none of Britten's early fame or opportunity, and only after *Grimes* proved that an English composer could have his work produced to the highest standard did Tippett begin *The Midsummer Marriage*. Working to his own libretto, Tippett laboured over the opera for six years, and it remained unperformed until 1955, when John Pritchard conducted the premiere, designed by Barbara Hepworth, at Covent Garden.

The opera aroused immediate controversy – largely on account of the libretto, which most found perversely obscure. The narrative concerns two couples' quest for sexual and physical fulfilment: Mark is engaged to Jenifer, daughter of the capitalist King Fisher, but she feels the need to find a greater understanding of herself before she can go ahead with the wedding. The two enter a cave in a mysterious clearing in the woods; they are followed by King Fisher, his secretary Bella, and her boyfriend Jack. After a series of rituals and dances, and the death of King Fisher, the couples emerge having found new understanding of themselves and each other, and are now ready to marry.

The Midsummer Marriage makes obvious reference to two earlier quest dramas: Mozart's *Die Zauberflöte*, in the way two contrasting sets of lovers undergo a trial – one spiritual, one psychological – before they can be united; and Shakespeare's *A Midsummer Night's Dream*, in the way that the world of the lovers overlaps with a supernatural world which may or may not be a dream. Tippett also borrowed from T. S. Eliot (whom Tippett asked for help with his text) and Jung, but the initial inspiration for the opera was a vision he had "of a wooded hilltop with a temple, where a warm and soft young man was being rebuffed by a cold and hard young woman . . . to such a degree that the collective, magical archetypes take charge – Jung's anima and animus – the girl, inflated by the latter, rises . . . to heaven, and the man, overwhelmed by the former, descends . . . to hell".

The Midsummer Marriage has remained the most popular of Tippett's operas, and it is easy to hear why. The sheer vigour and richness of the score is a wonder and, more clearly than the words, it conveys a sense of transcendence, at times reaching extraordinary heights of ecstatic lyricism. Reflecting the beauty of English summertime, Tippett's music is determinedly tonal and lyrical, with its roots planted firmly in the English pastoral tradition – indeed the long, slow-moving melodies often suggest Elgar in the way luscious harmonies are used to maximize spiritual intensity. It is true that Tippett often adds more and more layers until the initial idea is smothered, but ultimately this is one of the most joyous of all post-war operas.

Recorded in 1971, this performance stands as one of Colin Davis's most lasting achievements. Resisting the temptation to wallow in the splendour of the writing, Davis's disciplined approach illuminates the often thickly Romantic orchestration. The orchestra and chorus are in ravishing form, and the A-list cast is no less excellent, with outstanding contributions from Alberto Remedios as Mark and Joan Carlyle as Jenifer. Made in the studio straight after a Covent Garden revival, this recording is notable throughout for its sincerity and confidence.

85

Michael Tippett

King Priam

Norman Bailey (Priam), Heather Harper (Hecuba), Thomas Allen (Hector), Felicity Palmer (Andromache); London Sinfonietta; David Atherton (conductor)

Chandos 9406/7; 2 CDs; full price

Tippett was not at all deterred by the initially negative response to his first opera, but his second, *King Priam*, marked a quite radical shift from the lyrical and celebratory to the bitter and clamorous. On the advice of theatre director Peter Brook, Tippett turned to an ancient legend, that of the fall of Troy. Again he wrote his own libretto, beginning the narrative with the birth of Paris, son of Queen Hecuba and King Priam. When Hecuba dreams that her son will cause the death of his father, Priam entrusts the boy to a shepherd. He grows up to fall in love with Helen, the wife of Menelaus of Sparta, which leads to war between the Greeks and the Trojans, and ultimately to the murder of Priam by Achilles' son, Neoptolemus.

It is a story and a landscape filled with the suffering and pain of seemingly arbitrary and pointless killing, but Tippett saw the tale in terms of the fundamental questions that he had begun to explore in his earlier work. Significantly he presents the story from the perspective of the losers, concentrating on the way choices have profound and far-reaching effects beyond the individual who made them. Tippett does not really question the basic premise of Greek tragedy – that the destiny of the individual is inescapable. Instead he anatomizes the struggle that each individual decision presents, discussing its moral dimensions in

Brechtian interludes that occur between each scene. There are no easy answers in *King Priam*, although the opera also highlights the fact that compassion and fellow-feeling are always present even in war. In the most powerful scene in the opera the warrior Achilles feels pity, if not remorse, when Priam supplicates him for the body of his son.

The most obvious musical difference between *The Midsummer Marriage* and *King Priam* is the way the lush and largely contrapuntal orchestral writing of the earlier work has been replaced by something leaner and more focused. But what hasn't changed is the way Tippett's abstract and poetical text is transformed, and at times overwhelmed, by music of searing intensity. The orchestra may have been divided into smaller units, rarely playing in its entirety, but the resulting clarity brilliantly spotlights the emotional character of each scene. In some instances Tippett allocates particular instrumental combinations for different characters, as in the sombre but sensual cello writing that he gives to Andromache, or the violin figure that is associated with Hecuba. But for characters of greater complexity – in particular Priam and Achilles – he employs a variety of musical signifiers. Achilles gets the most lyrical moment in the whole opera, the guitar-accompanied "O rich-soiled land", and also the most chilling when – hearing of Patroclus' death – he puts on his armour and gives forth his terrible war cry. Priam, who is sung by a baritone, has a vocal style which is predominantly hard and declamatory but he also has moments of increasing serenity until by the end of the opera his music suggests a kind of inner peace.

David Atherton's 1981 recording boasts the cream of British singing talent, and at least three of Tippett's favourite performers. Norman Bailey brings both authority and vulnerability to the role of Priam, and Robert Tear makes a commanding Achilles. Heather Harper and Felicity Palmer are vocally sumptuous as Hecuba and Andromache, and Thomas Allen and Philip Langridge make distinguished appearances as Hector and Paris. The extraordinary tension of Tippett's score is brought out by Atherton with energy and panache, and the London Sinfonietta play with an almost chamber-like subtlety of expression.

86

Giuseppe Verdi

Rigoletto

Renato Bruson (Rigoletto), Edita Gruberová (Gilda), Neil Shicoff (The Duke of Mantua); Santa Cecilia Chorus and Orchestra; Giuseppe Sinopoli (conductor)

Philips 462 158-2PM2; 2 CDs; mid-price

Born into one of the most exciting periods in Italian musical history, Giuseppe Verdi reached maturity in the 1840s, when things had begun to look bleak: Rossini was in retirement, Bellini was dead and Donizetti was dying. Over the next fifty years, through the composition of nearly thirty operas, Verdi revitalized Italian music, giving it an identity as strong as that created for German music by Wagner. Arguably his most popular work is *Rigoletto*, which was based on Victor Hugo's play *Le Roi s'amuse* and promptly banned by the Venetian censor for its "disgusting immorality and obscene triviality" and for its inflammatory depiction of royalty. To get round this problem Verdi and his librettist Piave transplanted the action from the court of François I to that of the anonymous Duke of Mantua. After this change the censor approved the first production on March 11, 1851.

Rigoletto revolves around the title role, a hunchbacked court jester. Rigoletto mocks Count Ceprano who, in revenge, abducts Rigoletto's daughter, Gilda, believing her to be the jester's lover. Gilda loves the lecherous Duke – whom Rigoletto blames for his daughter's abduction. He engages the hitman Sparafucile to murder the Duke, but the assassin's sister Maddalena also loves the Duke, and persuades Sparafucile to spare the Duke and, instead, turn his knife on the next person to walk into their inn. Tragically, this is Gilda. Believing the body in the sack to be the Duke's, Rigoletto delights in his victory. Tearing open the sack, however, he discovers his dying daughter.

The libertine anti-hero, the guileless heroine, the evil assassin and the tragic jester are among the most vivid creations in all opera, thanks largely to Verdi's unflaggingly brilliant music. The tenor Duke's "La donna e mobile" (Women are fickle) might be the best-known moment, but the whole of *Rigoletto* is a parade of highlights, reaching a peak with the Act III quartet "Bella figlia dell'amore" (Fair daughter of love), in which all three protagonists plus Maddalena express their contrary emotions through a song of exquisite tenderness. *Rigoletto* overturns many of the formulas of Italian opera: it has a brief prelude rather than a full-blown overture; the chorus is all male; and there are no entrance arias, ensemble finales or conventional recitatives. Characters are not delineated in a single self-proclaiming aria, but are unfolded and explored over the course of the entire opera. And the entire opera is bound together by the figure of Rigoletto himself (a baritone), described by Verdi as "grossly deformed and absurd but inwardly passionate and full of love." Mocked for his deformity, but revelling in the humiliation of others, Rigoletto is a man of corrupted nobility whose paradoxes are illuminated in a series of impassioned songs and intense encounters. This opera's musical sophistication – its complex harmony, for instance, and its sinister orchestration (notably the storm of Act III) – always serves the portrayal of character, and in Rigoletto Verdi created a heartbreakingly tormented central figure.

Sinopoli's 1984 recording of *Rigoletto* is his finest of an Italian opera. The timing is brilliantly if eccentrically handled, with episodes of low tension suddenly erupting into moments of frenzied energy. Only one of the three leads is Italian, but the performance is sumptuously Italianate, with the under-rated American tenor Neil Shicoff in glowing form as the Duke and the Czech soprano Edita Gruberová a memorably gentle Gilda. Bruson is a magnificently voiced jester, and the whole is superbly recorded. Unfortunately, there is no libretto, although a detailed synopsis is provided.

87

Giuseppe Verdi

Il Trovatore

Franco Bonisolli (Manrico), Leontyne Price (Leonora), Piero Cappuccilli (Conte di Luna), Elena Obraztova (Azucena); Berlin Chorus; Berlin Philharmonic Orchestra; Herbert von Karajan (conductor)

EMI CMS7 69311-2; 2 CDs; mid-price

Rigoletto confirmed Verdi as Italy's most successful composer, a status that owed much to his ability to get the text as well as the music right. It is odd, then, that he immediately began work on one of the most famously rotten librettos of the nineteenth century – *Il Trovatore* (The Troubadour). It is the greatest testament to Verdi's genius as a composer that he managed to turn such unpromising material into one of the finest operas of the nineteenth century.

The plot is the sort of thing that gives opera a bad name. Many years before "curtain-up" the infant son of Count di Luna became ill after coming into contact with a gypsy, who was then burned at the stake. As revenge, the gypsy's daughter, Azucena, abducted di Luna's child, whom she intended to kill. Unfortunately, she killed her own son instead, which required her to raise di Luna's as her own. The opera tells how di Luna's surviving son has grown up to continue the search for his brother, all the time persecuting the gypsies, Azucena and her son Manrico – the troubadour of the title. After much revelation and counter-revelation, and the introduction of the love-interest Leonora, di Luna kills Manrico, only to be informed by the dying Azucena that he has murdered his long-lost brother.

Il Trovatore is packed with crowd-pleasing solo turns, big choruses, thrilling climaxes and complex ensemble finales – and, unlike *Rigoletto*, it requires next to no acting ability. Crucially, however, as Caruso remarked, it does demand "the four greatest singers in the world". *Il Trovatore* is a roller-coaster of frenetic passions, in which the lyrical episodes are there to provide a bridge between histrionics and more histrionics. Manrico is a textbook heroic tenor, whose character is distilled in the Act III cabaletta, "Di quella pira l'orrendo foco" (The horrible flames of that pyre), an act-ending show-stopper that concludes with an amazing high C. Verdi did not actually write this note into the aria, but the tenor Enrico Tamberlik, with Verdi's permission, stuck it onto the end, and it has now become a challenge that no tenor would dare shirk. The opera's other main focus is Azucena – perhaps the greatest mezzo-soprano role in Italian opera. From her Act I monologue "Strida la vampa" (The flames are roaring) to the chilling duet with Manrico "Condotta ell'era in ceppi" (They dragged her in bonds), this role provides career-making opportunities.

Wonderfully tuneful music occurs throughout the opera – perhaps the most famous episode is sung by the chorus of gypsies who, in Act II, get to pound their anvils in time with the music. But the most moving passages are created through dialogue, notably the Act IV "Miserere" duet between Manrico and Leonora, in which she sings to the imprisoned troubadour above a chorus of praying monks, and the final exchanges between the lovers, beginning with a fearsome outburst from the tenor. It is moments such as these that raise *Il Trovatore* way above the level of period-costume melodrama.

The finest all-round *Il Trovatore* is Karajan's thunderous 1977 account for EMI, recorded in the wake of a Salzburg Festival production. Bonisolli's Manrico might lack the electrifying ring that Corelli or del Monaco brought to the role, and Cappuccilli is a somewhat faceless di Luna, yet the overall performance will leave you breathless. Karajan's tempi are spectacular, and the orchestra and chorus are martial in their precision, but the highlights are Price's glowing Leonora and Obraztsova's forthright Azucena. The close recording underlines Karajan's typically percussive approach but the prevailing impression is one of extravagance.

88

Giuseppe Verdi

La Traviata

Angela Gheorghiu (Violetta), Frank Lopardo (Alfredo), Leo Nucci (Germont); Covent Garden Chorus and Orchestra; Georg Solti (conductor)

Decca 448 119-2; 2 CDs; full price

Verdi spent much of his time between 1847 and 1852 in Paris, where he may well have seen the first run of Alexandre Dumas' *La dame aux camélias*. With *La Traviata* (The Fallen Woman), the opera that came out of Dumas' play, Verdi moved from *Trovatore's* world of hot-blooded historical drama to something approximating to contemporary social realism, albeit glamorous upper-crust realism. Composed to a commission from La Fenice opera house in Venice, this tale of familial strife and disease-blighted love inevitably ran into trouble with the conservative censors, but the theatre's high-ranking contacts ensured that the only revision was the transplanting of the action from the present day to 1700. The first performance of *La Traviata* in 1853 was one of Verdi's few failures. The soprano creating the title role of the consumptive Violetta was the size of a bus, causing much laughter, while the baritone creating Germont shouted his way through the character's largely elegiac music. It was not long, however, before the opera was counted among the composer's most popular works, and it is today the most frequently performed and extensively recorded of Verdi's operas.

La Traviata is the ultimate weepie. The wealthy courtesan Violetta, who is suffering from tuberculosis, is introduced to an admirer, Alfredo. They fall in love and, though unmarried, take an apartment together. The scandal prompts Alfredo's father,

Germont, to visit the apartment while Alfredo is away. He begs Violetta to leave his son, as the shame is threatening the success of his daughter's wedding. She does as he asks. Alfredo rejects her, but some weeks later he learns of her sacrifice from his father and races to her rooms, only to find her at death's door. He begs her not to die, but after staggering to her feet she drops dead.

Although it contains its share of choruses (famously the "champagne chorus") and set-pieces (there are two party scenes), *La Traviata* is, in essence, a chamber opera. There are only three important characters – one of whom, Germont, does not appear until nearly an hour into the work – and each role is constructed to play off the others, raising the tension to the tragic pitch of the final scene. The economy of Verdi's writing is evident from the start: in contrast to, say, *Rigoletto* or *Trovatore*, very little actually happens during the first act and yet, starting with the prelude's ethereal portrayal of Violetta, the music conveys an amazing range of emotions. Violetta's exchanges with Alfredo establish their differing characters through the simplest of phrases (Alfredo languid and civilized, Violetta effervescent and fickle), while Violetta's concluding showpiece, "Sempre, libera" (Always free), is one of the greatest psychological portrayals in Italian opera. Constructed to maximize emotional impact without resorting to raucousness, *La Traviata* is the Verdi opera that is likeliest to make converts of the uninitiated. That is what Verdi meant when, asked some years later which of his operas he liked best, he replied, "Speaking as a professional, *Rigoletto*, as an amateur, *La Traviata*."

Violetta was the role that established the international reputation of Angela Gheorghiu, and this 1992 recording shows what the fuss is all about – she has a gorgeous voice, but like Callas she does much more with that voice than merely convey the notes. She acts with every inflection. Her Alfredo is the fledgling superstar Frank Lopardo, whose youthful and warm voice is one of the few great hopes for modern Italian tenor singing. Leo Nucci is a bland Germont, but the octogenarian Georg Solti gives a splendidly vital and well-paced account of the score. Marvellously recorded.

89

Giuseppe Verdi

La Forza del Destino

Maria Callas (Leonora), Richard Tucker (Don Alvaro), Carlo Tagliabue (Don Carlo); La Scala Chorus and Orchestra; Tullio Serafin (conductor)

EMI CDS7 47581-8; 3 CDs; full price

La Forza del Destino (The Force of Destiny) is a work that stands alone amid Verdi's output. The abstract title is a clue to its singularity: *La Forza* is populated by people whose actions seem to be governed by something other than the imperatives of character. In a work which might more justly be titled "The Force of Coincidence", each of the three leading characters occupies an isolated place in the drama's universe, and tragedy ensues whenever their paths cross. So loose is the structure that Leonora does not even appear during Act III and she only returns to the opera for the final scene – just in time for her death. What cohesion the opera possesses comes from the use of leitmotif, such as the "Fate theme" – first heard as a pugilistic brass call at the beginning of the overture – and the haunting allusions to Leonora's Act II prayer. Otherwise, the opera rambles from highlight to highlight.

The rambling story begins with the elopement of Don Alvaro and Leonora, during which they are ambushed by her father, the Marquis of Calatrava. In the ensuing struggle the Marquis is killed. As he dies he curses his daughter. Her brother, Carlo, chases her and Alvaro around Spain, bent on revenge. Carlo and Alvaro – neither knowing the identity of the other – become friends, only to become enemies when Carlo discovers a portrait of Leonora in Alvaro's pocket. While Carlo continues his pursuit of Leonora, Alvaro joins a monastery; Leonora also gives herself up to God, but chooses to live in a cave as a hermit. Five years later all three meet by accident at Leonora's cave, where Alvaro kills Carlo who, as he is dying, stabs his sister.

Musically, the chief strength of *La forza del destino* is the tenor role of Alvaro. Verdi provided him with an extraordinary stream of expressive melody, the high points of which are the colossal recitative and aria "O tu che in seno agl'angeli" (Oh you who dwell among the angels) at the beginning of Act III, and the ensuing duet with Carlo, "Solenne in quest'ora" (You must swear to me). The baritone role of Don Carlo is another of Verdi's declamatory bad-guys, while Leonora is an extravagantly tragic figure, a characteristic accentuated through the doom-laden minor-key properties of much of the music that surrounds her. When tranquillity seems about to dawn, at the close of the second act, the forbidding music that follows her ensemble "La Vergine degli angeli" (Our Lady of the Angels) hints that her rest is only temporary. In Act IV, her reverential prayer "Pace, pace, mio dio" (Peace, peace, oh my God), with its sweeping phrases set above an undulating accompaniment, glows with a radiance that gives her an almost angelic demeanour. For a moment it appears as if her prayers have been answered – but, once again, fate catches up. As shouting is heard offstage, it becomes immediately clear that not even a hermit can escape the path of destiny.

The recording that best captures the febrile character of *La forza del destino* was conducted for EMI in 1954 by Tullio Serafin with a cast of rare perfection. Maria Callas was at her peak with this benchmark portrayal of Leonora: this is one of those roles she was born to play, and her kaleidoscopic range of inflection brings real tragedy to this portrayal. Richard Tucker gave no better performance on record than this: his vibrant, Italianate tenor brings a superb rush to Alvaro's music. Carlo Tagliabue made few recordings, but his portrayal of Carlo is perfectly in keeping with the high melodrama of *La forza del destino*. The singers are strongly supported throughout by Serafin, who keeps the tempi brisk, and the orchestral backdrop colourful.

90

Giuseppe Verdi

Don Carlo

José Carreras (Don Carlos), Mirella Freni (Elisabeth), Agnes Baltsa (Princess Eboli); Berlin Opera Chorus; Berlin Philharmonic Orchestra; Herbert von Karajan (conductor)

EMI CMS7 69304-2; 3 CDs; mid-price

During the 1860s Verdi spent a great deal of time in Paris, where his exalted status was confirmed by a commission from the Paris Opéra. The source he chose for this new opera was Schiller's *Don Carlos*, a play that takes a proto-Hollywood attitude towards the facts in dramatizing the life of a Habsburg prince who in reality was an epileptic psychopath, feared and loathed by all around him. Verdi and his librettists followed Schiller in painting the monster as a man of honour, torn between his responsibility to the downtrodden and his love for an ideal woman. He even scored Carlos as a tenor – the voice of all romantic heroes.

As you might expect of an opera drawn from a Schiller play, the plot of *Don Carlos* turned out to be more than merely complicated, but the bare bones are as follows. Spain and France are at war. Peace is promised if Don Carlos, the heir to Philip II's throne, marries Elisabeth de Valois. Carlos is delighted (breaking the heart of his friend Rodrigo, who is in love with her), but Philip decides to marry her himself, causing a rift between father and son. This bleeds into public life when Carlos opposes Philip and the Grand Inquisitor's persecutions of the Flemish. Carlos and Elisabeth continue to meet in secret but Philip (aided by Princess Eboli, Elisabeth's spurned lady-in-waiting) tracks them down to the monastery of San Yuste, where the ghost of Carlos's grandfather, Charles V, leads Carlos to safety.

At over four hours in length, the five-act *Don Carlos* was too much for the Parisian public: "Verdi is no longer Italian, he is following Wagner" commented Bizet. In response Verdi produced an Italian version, dropping the "s" from the title and cutting a lot of music, including the whole of the first act. Although it still suffers from some of the ailments of its time (excessive length, otiose dance music and too many big choruses), this edition (premiered in 1884, seventeen years after the Paris premiere), is on the whole preferable, for it accentuates the intimacy of its finest music and of its central drama, in which respect it clearly resembles *Otello*. Even more than *Otello*, however, *Don Carlo* is remarkable for its contrasts: its manic oscillations between introspection and melodrama make this Verdi's most intense and restive opera. A sensational example of this switchback quality occurs during the confrontation between Rodrigo and Philip at the end of the second act when their talk of peace is ripped apart by Rodrigo's savage exclamation: "A horrible, dreadful peace", the words being roared above low brass and thunderous chords. Of course, such declamatory episodes are offset by Verdi's always remarkable lyric skill, and Don Carlos's tenor, Elisabeth's soprano and the bass/baritone trio of Rodrigo, Philip II and the Grand Inquisitor are each assigned some unforgettably poignant melodies.

The finest recording of *Don Carlo*, and one of the greatest operatic recordings ever made, is Karajan's 1978 performance for EMI. The intensity of his conducting makes this an unbelievably potent experience. He gets the huge Berlin chorus and orchestra to produce waves of rich, bass-heavy sound, providing an amazingly colourful backdrop for his almost perfect cast. The young Carreras is in magnificent voice, and he is easily the most impressive Carlos on record; soprano Mirella Freni and mezzo Agnes Baltsa spark off each other as Elisabeth and Eboli, and Ghiaurov and Raimondi achieve almost delirious levels of tension as Philip II and the Grand Inquisitor.

91

Giuseppe Verdi

Aida

Renata Tebaldi (Aida), Carlo Bergonzi (Radamès), Giulietta Simionato (Amneris); Vienna Singverein; Vienna Philharmonic Orchestra; Herbert von Karajan (conductor)

Decca 414 087-2DM3; 3 CDs; mid-price

In November 1869 Khedive Ismail, the ruler of Egypt, announced plans for the opening of a new opera house in Cairo as part of the celebrations surrounding the opening of the Suez Canal. He asked Verdi to compose an "inaugural hymn" for its opening night, which was planned for November 1870; Verdi wasn't keen on the idea, but in April 1870 he proposed an opera, *Aida*, on an ancient Egyptian subject. Thanks partly to the outbreak of war between France and Prussia, Verdi failed to deliver in time, and the opera house opened with a performance of *Rigoletto*. The premiere of *Aida* was given in Egypt on Christmas Eve, 1871.

Verdi went to great lengths to imbue his work with authentic local colour, studying Egyptian history, geography and religion, and he even commissioned replicas of ancient Egyptian flutes and trumpets. For all these efforts, however, the setting of *Aida* is just a backdrop to a story that would work in almost any historical context. The Ethiopian people have begun to fight back against their Egyptian oppressors. The Ethiopian army, led by King Amonasro, has crossed the border into Egypt, where the Egyptian commander, Radamès, is chosen to led the Egyptian defence. Radamès wishes to marry Aida, an Ethiopian slave girl assigned to the Pharaoh's daughter, Amneris, who is also in love with Radamès. Naturally, Amneris despises Aida and, through much trickery, uses her to expose Radamès as a traitor. Amneris offers Radamès the Pharaoh's pardon if he will renounce Aida. Having refused all offers of help, he and Aida are buried alive in a tomb.

Aida may be famous for its huge choruses – and the Act I triumphal march, "Gloria all'egito" (Glory of Egypt), is about as huge as choruses get – but *Aida* is a psychological drama rather than a cast-of-thousands show, and its tone is considerably more intimate than its best-known moment suggests. The opera opens discreetly, with a prelude of softly spun strings, with which Verdi brilliantly evokes both the Egyptian scene and the tormented psyches of the protagonists. And although the opera's first aria, the tenor Radamès' punishingly difficult "Celeste Aida" (Heavenly Aida), is introduced by a blaring trumpet fanfare, this bombastic flourish is, typically for this opera, a setting against which the hero's melancholy song appears yet more intensely personal. Verdi gave most of the work's finest music to Aida herself, a dramatic soprano role through which Verdi continued his preoccupation with the parent–child relationship (cf *Rigoletto, Il Trovatore, La Traviata* and *Don Carlos*). Riven between her love for Radamès and her responsibility to her father, she commands the spotlight with two great arias in Act I ("Ritorna vincitor!" – Return victorious) and Act III ("O patria mia" – O my country), and a series of powerful duets, culminating with the heartbreaking entombment scene. The final moments of Aida and Radamès bear an obvious similarity to the conclusion of Wagner's *Tristan und Isolde*, but the mood could not be more different: here the music is amazingly calm, with each secure in the knowledge that, through death, they will be united forever.

As with so many of Decca's opera recordings of the 1950s, Karajan's 1959 *Aida*, with Tebaldi and Bergonzi in the principal roles, is a classic interpretation, remarkable for the warmth and conviction of the singing and the intensity of the conducting. Tebaldi and Bergonzi in full song is the aural equivalent of a warm bath, Simionato's Amneris is fantastically exciting and Cornell MacNeil makes more of the worthy Amonasro than most. The fine sound and opulent Viennese orchestra add considerably to this recording's great appeal.

92

Giuseppe Verdi

Otello

Placido Domingo (Otello), Cheryl Studer (Desdemona), Sergei Leiferkus
(Iago), Ramon Vargas (Cassio); Paris Opéra-Bastille Chorus and
Orchestra; Myung-Whun Chung (conductor)

Deutsche Grammophon 439 805-2GH2; 2 CDs; full price

After completing *Aida* Verdi
wrote no new opera for fifteen
years. Like Rossini, who also
retired in his prime, Verdi had
clearly had enough of the stage.
Unlike Rossini, however, Verdi
was tempted out of retirement.
Arrigo Boito, with whom the
composer had collaborated on a
revision of his opera *Simon
Boccanegra* in 1881, persistently suggested subjects for one final
work, all of which Verdi rejected on account of his advanced
years. But when Boito proposed a setting of Shakespeare's
Othello, and set to work reducing the play's 3500 lines to a more
manageable 800, Verdi could resist no more. He began work on
the score in 1884, and the first performance took place in 1887 –
an internationally reported event which nearly every critic
reported as the crowning achievement of Verdi's career, a status it
continues to enjoy.

The depiction of Otello's decline epitomizes the sophistication of Verdi's later operas. Stravinsky once quipped that it
would be a good idea to throw all Verdi's best arias into a single, two-hour show, but with *Otello* every line plays a part in
the development of the drama. Whereas he might previously
have charted Otello's demise through a series of set numbers,
each detailing a step in his downfall, here the emotional complexion changes within every episode. During his harrowing

Act III monologue "Dio, mi potevi scagliar tutti i mali" (God, thou couldst have rained upon my head), for example, Otello moves from half-sobbing despair via nervous regret to a bestial eruption of anger. Similarly, his final monologue, "Niun mi tema" (Would you dare), is full of rapid mood shifts, ending with one of the most poignant death scenes in all opera. To further *Otello*'s fluency Verdi relied on a limited but brilliantly effective palette of motifs (most potently the "Kiss" motif that crops up initially during the Act I love duet, and again in each of the following two acts, culminating in its resolution during the death scene), using the orchestral backdrop to anticipate, mirror and respond to the characters' turmoil at every step. As might be expected, the title role dominates throughout. Since the first performance in 1884 it has represented the peak of the dramatic tenor's repertoire, and such is the difficulty of the role – which ranges from low baritone to high tenor – that singers have devoted their entire careers to its mastery. Mario del Monaco, for example, sang the role nearly six hundred times in twenty years.

Myung-Whun Chung's reading of *Otello* upset a lot of reviewers when it was released in 1993, primarily because he took what was deemed to be an unduly creative approach to Verdi's markings. And it's true that his tempi and phrasing are, to say the least, unconventional. However, his choices usually sound like right choices, and he drives the drama to an unprecedented frenzy, with a vast dynamic and expressive range. The balance of soloists and orchestra is expertly maintained too. The title role is taken by Placido Domingo, who has effectively established a monopoly of the part since the 1970s. This is his third recording of it, and after a hurried "Esultate" – Otello's opening cry of triumph – he settles into what turns out to be one of the greatest performances of his career, even if his vocal resources are not what they used to be. Studer makes a somewhat brittle Desdemona, but she gives a touchingly vulnerable reading of the famous "Willow Song". The obviously Russian Leiferkus is a vulpine Iago, and easily the most interesting Iago to feature on a Domingo recording.

93

Richard Wagner

Der fliegende Holländer

Bernd Weikl (Dutchman), Cheryl Studer (Senta), Placido Domingo (Erik), Peter Seiffert (Helmsman); Choir and Orchestra of the Deutsche Opera, Berlin; Giuseppe Sinopoli (conductor)

Deutsche Grammophon 437 778-2; 2 CDs; full price

With *Der fliegende Holländer* (The Flying Dutchman) Wagner began the transformation of opera into what he termed the *Gesamtkunstwerk* – the total work of art. In place of conventional divisions between arias, ensembles, accompaniment and so forth, each component was now subsumed into what Wagner called "a musical and poetic unit, entirely homogeneous". For the first time, everything that happened on the stage and in the pit, from the instrumentation and harmony to the stage movement and lighting, was to be focused by the composer's dramatic purpose. Wagner marked almost every bar of this score with some instruction – nothing was to be left to chance.

With the exception of the first instalment of *Der Ring*, the *Dutchman* is the shortest and most direct of Wagner's mature operas, but it can still be an overpowering experience for anyone for whom opera means Mozart or Rossini. The narrative is relatively eventless but heavy with symbolic meaning. The Dutchman is condemned to sail the seas for eternity, unless redeemed by the love of a "woman faithful unto death", an ideal embodied by Senta who, though loved by the huntsman Erik, falls for the Dutchman. When he mistakenly believes her to be unfaithful he leaves, driving Senta to suicide – and their eternal union. Wagner's score gives this philosophical drama an appropriately oceanic fluidity, primarily through atmospheric orchestration which frequently relegates the voices – even the Dutchman's tormented baritone – to an almost supplementary role, reversing the traditional relationship in which the orchestra accompanies the voice. There's a supernatural hue to parts of this work, a feature that relates back to the work of early Romantics such as Weber, but nature (particularly the sea) is the all-pervasive influence. The overture (in which the pivotal struggle between damnation and redemption is first portrayed), the storm music, the Steersman's tenor song and the "Sailor's Chorus" all evoke the implacability of the elements, which in turn mirror the passions of the characters. Like so much else in Wagner's operas, humanity and nature are indivisible in *Der fliegende Holländer*.

In this opera many of Wagner's key ideas are developed extensively for the first time. Wagner was greatly taken by the notion of man's redemption through the love and devotion of an "ideal woman" (his words), and he fused this idea with the idea of Christ's sacrifice to develop the typically Wagnerian concept of the "love-death", in which the surrender of life itself was the consummating act of love. The ending of the *Dutchman* is Wagner's draft of what was to be a pivotal concept in the *Ring* cycle, and the very raison d'etre of *Tristan und Isolde*. The strong-willed Senta is a sister to the "ideal" Isolde and Brünnhilde, while the Dutchman himself is conceived as a blood-brother to the Wandering Jew, whose burden it is to carry the guilt for the murder of Christ – a stereotype that would surface again forty years later in *Parsifal*. Finally, of course, the Dutchman is also the Artist: with *Der fliegende Holländer* the twenty-nine-year-old composer erected the first great monument to the cult of himself.

Giuseppe Sinopoli is a controversial conductor, but his recording of the *Dutchman* is tremendous stuff. His approach is typically fluid, as is his cast, with the sweet and effortless voices of Cheryl Studer as Senta, Placido Domingo as Erik and Peter Seiffert as the Helmsman. A more declamatory style is evident throughout Bernd Weikl's resonant, uncommonly noble portrayal of the Dutchman. The Berlin orchestra and chorus are in glowing form and the recording is state of the art, with a remarkably vital balance between orchestra and soloists.

94

Richard Wagner

Lohengrin

Peter Seiffert (Lohengrin), Falk Struckmann (Telramund), Emily Magee (Elsa), Deborah Polaski (Ortrud); Berlin State Opera Chorus; Berlin State Opera Orchestra; Daniel Barenboim (conductor)

Teldec 3984-21484-2; 2 CDs; full price

The inspiration for *Lohengrin* came to Wagner while sitting in his bath: leaping from the water, he ran to his desk and in one unbroken rush he wrote a thirty-page prose sketch of the score and its staging. The first performance was conducted by Franz Liszt in 1850 with an orchestra of just over forty musicians, as opposed to the one hundred deployed for its premiere in Wagner's theatre in Bayreuth. That Liszt could get away with such a small orchestra says much about *Lohengrin*, for this is Wagner's most transparent work.

The opera is set in tenth-century Brabant. In the hope of securing the succession to the throne, Count Telramund accuses Elsa of having murdered her brother Gottfried. King Henry orders trial by combat between Telramund and Elsa's champion. A mysterious knight, Lohengrin, arrives, defeats the count and marries Elsa. Telramund and Ortrud then conspire to undermine Elsa's faith in her husband. They succeed and, defying Lohengrin's wishes, she demands to know his name and origin. He tells her that he is a knight of the Holy Grail, permitted to live among men so long as his identity remains unknown. He bids farewell to Elsa and as he leaves the missing Gottfried returns.

Telling a stirring tale in which good and evil battle it out against a background of royal pageantry and intrigue, *Lohengrin* is in some respects the most accessible of all Wagner's operas. The narrative is underpinned by music that has the tone of an even-tempered narrative all the way through from the haunting orchestral Prelude. Cohesion is reinforced through a highly developed system of leitmotifs: whereas in previous operas a musical signature had been called upon to remind the audience of a character or episode, Wagner was now using the device to illustrate abstract ideas. These have yet to reach the sophistication of the *Ring*, in which an interval or harmonic progression might carry dramatic significance, but they nonetheless provide a solid foundation for the narrative.

There are some outstanding moments – notably the rumbustious Prelude to Act III, the beautiful Bridal Chorus (which quickly found its way, to Wagner's amusement, into churches across the world), and Ortrud's magnificent call for vengeance in Act II – but *Lohengrin* doesn't pack the emotional punch of his later work. Wagner intended *Lohengrin* to be more like a religious ceremony than a theatrical event, and his deployment of the orchestra sustains a suitably devotional tone, albeit with the vivacity of the instrumentation often compensating for the demure pace (groups of violins are set against each other, while the woodwind is treated as a group of individual voices). In its atmosphere and subject, *Lohengrin* foreshadows *Parsifal*, albeit in far simpler form, and there are many Wagner fans who prefer the intimacy and reserve of *Lohengrin* to the fireworks of the *Ring*.

Lohengrin never moves out of its opening time signature (4/4), which can lead to draggy performances, but Daniel Barenboim's 1998 recording is one of the fleetest on record, and he creates a marvellous sense of urgency. The Prelude to Act I has never been more haunting, the Prelude to Act III never more explosive, and these contrasts typify a performance that is defined by its drama and energy. Peter Seiffert is an ideal Lohengrin: his tenor is full and even, and he captures the character's fusion of nobility and melancholy to perfection. Emily Magee is less suited to the role of Elsa, sounding rather too much like the heavyweight Deborah Polaski (Ortrud); otherwise, the production is exceptional in every department, and confirms Barenboim's status as the greatest living Wagner conductor.

95

Richard Wagner

Tristan und Isolde

Wolfgang Windgassen (Tristan), Birgit Nilsson (Isolde), Christa Ludwig
(Brangäne), Martti Talvela (King Marke); Bayreuth Festival Chorus,
Bayreuth Festival Orchestra; Karl Böhm (conductor)

Deutsche Grammophon 449 772-2GOR3; 3 CDs; mid-price

Wagner wrote to Liszt in 1854:
"Since I have never enjoyed the
real happiness of love in my life, I
want to erect another monument
to this most beautiful of dreams in
which love will be properly sated
from beginning to end." *Tristan
und Isolde* was the fulfilment of
that ambition. Shocked by its bla-
tant sexuality, men at the first per-
formance removed their womenfolk from the Munich theatre,
and a priest was seen to cross himself before fleeing in horror.
Wagner himself was terrified by his own opera, writing to his
lover Mathilde Wesendonck: "This Tristan is turning into something fearful! That last act!!! . . . I'm afraid the opera will be forbidden . . . only mediocre performances can save me.
Completely good ones are bound to drive people mad."

For his plot, Wagner turned to a thirteenth-century epic poem
by Gottfried von Strassburg. The Irish princess Isolde is on her
way to Cornwall, and marriage to King Marke. She is escorted
by Tristan, who earlier killed her betrothed Morald in battle. She
orders her attendant, Brangäne, to prepare a poison, but
Brangäne substitutes a love potion and when Tristan and Isolde
drink from the bottle they fall madly in love. When their liaison
is discovered by King Marke, Tristan is mortally wounded and
dies in Isolde's arms. Isolde proclaims her eternal love for Tristan
and falls dead beside him.

Less a tale than a psychodrama, *Tristan* is an unprecedentedly symphonic opera, a huge triple-movement construction within which every pause and silence serves a dramatic function, intensifying the claustrophobically erotic atmosphere. Despite its great length this is a streamlined work. The cast is small, with only two major characters, the music describes a unbroken arc in which little action occurs, and the entire work hangs on a single chord progression that remains unresolved from the prelude until Isolde's "Transfiguration", commonly known as the "Liebestod" (Love-death). Dozens of motifs (between forty and sixty, depending on how you analyse them) bind the piece together and project the flux of emotions: every chord of *Tristan* draws the audience into the lovers' all-annihilating passion. The atmosphere becomes almost unbearable during the frenetic love duet of Act II, in which the music grows ever more hysterical until, some thirty minutes into the duet, the graphically simulated coitus is interrupted by King Marke and one of the most fearsome discords in all music. Dragging tonality to the most extreme limits, Wagner created a musical narrative in which the harmony is richer, the melodies are longer and the counterpoint is more complex than in any other nineteenth-century opera. Schoenberg credited *Tristan* with "the emancipation of the dissonance", and it is a measure of Wagner's genius that he anticipated the radicalism of Schoenberg and his cohorts way back in 1856 – less than thirty years after the death of Beethoven.

Karl Böhm was capable of boring the pants off any audience, especially as he got older, but this live 1966 Bayreuth production captured him in fearsome form: such is the pace he takes it at that he fits each of the three acts onto a single CD, which no other conductor manages. The barnstorming performance comes from the mighty Birgit Nilsson, whose steam-whistle soprano rips through the score. Wolfgang Windgassen's tenor was beginning to thin out by 1966 but he is a superb stylist, and he keeps going – which, considering Böhm's relentless direction, is a miracle. Christa Ludwig's vibrant Brangäne is exquisite while Eberhard Waechter and Martti Talvela round off a vocally sumptuous, theatrically intense, perfectly recorded performance.

96

Richard Wagner

Der Ring des Nibelungen

Various artists; Bayreuth Festival Chorus and Orchestra; Karl Böhm (conductor)

Philips 446 057-2PB14; 14 CDs; budget price

There have been few artists as ambitious as Richard Wagner, and fewer still with the single-minded determination to devote more than a quarter of a century to a single work. He began *Der Ring des Nibelungen* (The Ring of the Nibelung) in 1848 and twenty-eight years later, having built his own theatre in which to present it, he oversaw the first complete production of the four operas that make up the fifteen-hour drama: *Das Rheingold*, *Die Walküre*, *Siegfried* and *Götterdämmerung*. It is the longest theatrical work regularly performed anywhere outside India, and its dramaturgical and logistical demands continue to present opera houses with unparalleled challenges. Wagner intended the *Ring* to "involve all life", and if it doesn't quite do that, it does offer inexhaustible scope for interpretation: different producers have successfully staged it as a Jungian psychodrama and as a parable of the collapse of capitalism.

Reduced to its barest elements, the *Ring* is a mythical parable of the consequences of greed. Numerous other themes recur throughout – the abuse of power, the immutability of fate, and the status of love as the "final true and knowing redeemer" – but it begins and ends in the shadow of avarice. The chain of events that lead to the downfall of the gods is begun by Wotan, who steals the power-giving Ring from the dwarf Alberich (who has fashioned it from gold stolen from the Rhinemaidens), in order to pay for the construction of Valhalla. With *Götterdämmerung* the drama comes full circle: Wotan's crime is redeemed by the death of the hero Siegfried and his lover Brünnhilde; the ring is returned to the Rhinemaidens, and Valhalla sinks beneath the waters from which the gold was stolen.

The *Ring* is an overwhelming musical experience, although it is by no means typified by its well-known highlights, such as *Die Walküre*'s "Ride of the Valkyries" or "Siegfried's Death" in *Götterdämmerung*. Rather, it is a work of huge variety and expressivity, in which there is as much introspection as bombast, and in which every major episode has ramifications throughout the subsequent drama. Indeed, the integration of the *Ring* is a staggering feat. Some two hundred harmonic and melodic themes, most of them derived from the simple wave-pattern that opens *Das Rheingold*, unite and direct every event, character and emotion, mutating through contact with each other in a process of constant re-invention.

For all this talk of high artistic purpose and achievement, it can't be too strongly stressed that the *Ring* is superlative entertainment, to use a word Wagner detested. The cycle is a thrilling ride through a self-contained universe. The ominous undulating music of the Rhine; the clangorous anvil-music of Nibelheim; the gods' march towards Valhalla; the "Magic Fire" music; the tragic-triumphant music of Siegfried's funeral march; Brünnhilde's immolation – these are just glimpses of the *Ring*'s treasure.

This set provides a perfect all-round introduction to the *Ring*, at low cost. Recorded in 1966/67 at Bayreuth, Karl Böhm's performance is remarkable for its energy and power. It is also the most consistent, with a uniformly outstanding cast, and if it has some of the drawbacks of a live set, then it comes with all the benefits too – not least the thrill of hearing the likes of Birgit Nilsson, James King, Wolfgang Windgassen and Theo Adam in full flow. The secondary casting is excellent, and the Bayreuth Orchestra, probably the finest outside Vienna in the 1960s, play like demons. The whole production has the sort of theatrical edge absolutely essential to this most theatrical of enterprises. There's no libretto, unfortunately, but there is a detailed synopsis.

97

Richard Wagner

Die Meistersinger von Nürnberg

Paul Schöffler (Hans Sachs), Günther Treptow (Walther), Hilde Gueden (Eva), Anton Dermota (David); Vienna State Opera Chorus; Vienna Philharmonic Orchestra; Hans Knappertsbusch (conductor)

Decca 440 057-2DM04; 4 CDs; mid-price

Having exhausted himself with *Tristan und Isolde*, Wagner began writing a comic opera, taking as his subject the Mastersingers. These societies thrived in Germany between the fourteenth and sixteenth centuries, and believed themselves to be the guardians of German musical tradition. Bearing in mind Wagner's obsessive nationalism, the appeal of such a theme is not difficult to understand, but beneath the banner-waving of *Die Meistersinger von Nürnberg* (both literally and implicitly) there lies a delicate love story, a sublime character study in the figure of Hans Sachs, and some delicious (if not always subtle) comedy, much of it directed at Beckmesser, a figure based loosely on Wagner's fiercest critic, the conservative Eduard Hanslick. Wagner himself appears in the guise of Walther von Stolzing, the opera's hero, who, like the composer, is both the champion of the new and the regenerator of tradition.

With a larger cast than any of his previous operas, *Die Meistersinger*'s narrative is also somewhat more involved (the third act alone is as long as *Das Rheingold*), but the elements are simple. Walther wishes to marry Eva, daughter of the blacksmith Pogner. For him to do so he must join the Mastersingers' guild and win their song contest. Eva is being courted by the town clerk, Beckmesser, who frustrates Walther's efforts to join the guild. When Walther and Eva try to elope they are stopped by

Hans Sachs, who sends Eva (whom he loves) to Pogner and takes Walther into his home. That night Walther dreams of a tune, for which, the following morning, Hans Sachs writes two stanzas. When Walther sings it, he wins both the contest and Eva's hand in marriage.

The music for *Die Meistersinger* is like chalk to *Tristan's* cheese. Where the earlier work is dark and heavily chromatic, *Meistersinger* is bright and largely diatonic, with a traditional bedrock of overtures, preludes, arias and choruses. Hans Sachs, the personification of Wagner's notions about the healing powers of art, sings some of the most poignant bass monologues in all opera, and Wagner memorably characterizes his weary resignation to his fate. Aside from Sachs' minor-key introversion, the opera is predominantly upbeat; Walther's four tenor arias (most famously the concluding "Prize Song"), the exquisite quintet (written to trump *Fidelio's* celebrated foursome) and the rip-roaring overture are irrepressibly affirmative creations. Aside from these highlights the opera is notable for its chorus work and the engaging use of Lutheran chorales, fugues and Bach-like counterpoint to generate a comfortably enveloping old-world atmosphere. Of course, there is in Wagner's blinkered reverence for German tradition a strong undercurrent of xenophobic triumphalism that makes *Meistersinger* unpalatable for many people. However, there is no denying the sweep and beauty of this most extraordinary work.

Hans Knappertsbusch made only a handful of studio recordings during his long life, but they are uniformly outstanding. This 1951 production of *Die Meistersinger* is an effortlessly lyrical interpretation and unusually light on its feet – Knappertsbusch is more often associated with weighty solemnity, as typified by his performances of *Parsifal*. Paul Schöffler is authoritative as Sachs, and even though the voice is not what it was, his absorption with the role is total. Günther Treptow gives an old-fashioned portrayal of Walther, producing some splendidly lachrymose tones, and Hilde Gueden swoons her way through the role of Eva, bringing an infectious Viennese élan to the great arches of melody. The Viennese orchestra is in splendid form and although the sound is mono this should not put you off what is an ideal set.

98

Richard Wagner

Parsifal

Jess Thomas (Parsifal), George London (Amfortas), Hans Hotter (Klingsor), Martti Talvela (Gurnemanz), Irene Dalis (Kundry); Bayreuth Festival Chorus and Orchestra; Hans Knappertsbusch (conductor)

Philips 416 390-2PH4; 4 CDs; full price

Parsifal is Wagner's most controversial opera. Deriving its text from Wolfram von Eschenbach's 24,000-line medieval poem *Parzival*, and many of its underlying ideas from Schopenhauer's thoughts on redemption through the rejection of the Self, Wagner created a pseudo-Christian stage ritual that is philosophically utterly corrupt. In conjunction with *Parsifal* Wagner published an essay titled "Heroism and Christianity", in which he argued that the Aryans, the "German leaders of mankind", evolved from the gods, while the "lesser races" (everyone else) descended from the apes. Wagner was disgusted by the notion of a religion founded on the worship of a Jew, and *Parsifal* can be seen as his attempt to re-invent the Christ figure in a more Germanic image. Even if the anti-Semitism were not there, there is still something unpalatable about the liturgical services that punctuate the drama and about the character of Kundry, a Mary Magdalene figure with an extra misogynistic spin, who presents a foil and motivation for the monastic knights. What makes *Parsifal* so problematic is that it is unquestionably a stupendous piece of music.

Amfortas, the head of the knights and Keeper of the Grail, is the mainspring of the action. He was once seduced by Kundry, a woman condemned to perpetual penance after mocking the crucified Christ, and was struck in the side by the evil magician

Klingsor with the spear that pierced Christ's side, leaving him with a never-healing wound. Parsifal – the "pure fool" who becomes "wise through compassion" – destroys Klingsor, retrieves the spear, baptizes Kundry and cures Amfortas.

More than any other Wagner operas, *Parsifal* brings words, music and drama into perfect communion. With its intimate play between leitmotif and language, its austerely choreographed stage action, and its slow-moving, contemplative music, *Parsifal* is an opera in which absolutely nothing is superfluous. The prevailing hushed atmosphere is established at the outset, through a sixteen-minute prelude in which the opera's three most resonant motifs are first heard – the climactic theme being the "Dresden Amen", a stirring cadence that dates back to the sixteenth century. Although it resembles *Tristan* in that the lengthy prelude establishes tensions that are released only at the opera's conclusion, *Parsifal* has nothing of *Tristan*'s impetuosity. Indeed, the use of chant-like themes for the chorus creates an air of monastic tranquillity, and even the carnality of Klingsor's Flower Maidens is of a passive, almost solipsistic kind.

Where *Tristan*, the *Ring* and *Meistersinger* show Wagner's imagination at its most complex, *Parsifal* returns to the mysterious uncertainties of *Lohengrin*, but with a far greater sense of gravity and inwardness. What sets the mood-painting of *Parsifal* apart from anything Wagner wrote before is the economy of its means and the use of silence as a positive element in the score. *Parsifal* is an exercise in suspension, relying more upon the accumulation of suggestion than the thrill of effect, and so anticipates the shifting, twilit world of Debussy's *Pelléas et Mélisande*.

This 1962 Bayreuth recording is a classic: the performances are faultless and the early stereo captures the extraordinarily beautiful Bayreuth sound perfectly. This is the second of Hans Knappertsbusch's recordings of the opera. It is generally lighter than the first, which is a definite advantage in music that often approaches stasis, and it is also better sung, with a magnificent Parsifal from Jess Thomas and a remarkably moving Amfortas from George London. Hans Hotter's Klingsor and Martti Talvela's Gurnemanz are just as fine, while Irene Dalis's Kundry, hurling caution to the wind, is the most compelling on disc.

99

Carl Maria von Weber

Der Freischütz

Rudolph Schock (Max), Elizabeth Grümmer (Agathe), Lisa Otto (Ännchen), Wilhelm Kohn (Caspar), Gottlob Frick (Ottokar); Berlin Deutsches Opera Chorus; Berlin Philharmonic Orchestra; Joseph Keilberth (conductor)

EMI CMS7 69342-2; 2 CDs; full price

Only one of Weber's operas is performed regularly, which gives little indication of his place in the history of German music. Within a few years of his death in 1826, aged just 39, he was widely acknowledged as the father of German Romantic opera, the creator of a body of work that crystallized a sense of national identity in much the same way as the music of Rossini gave voice to the Italian self-image. Yet Weber's early operas barely anticipated the splendour of his sixth, *Der Freischütz* (The Marksman), nor its colossal success. As Weber wrote in his diary after the first performance in 1821: "Greater enthusiasm there cannot be, and I tremble to think of the future, for it is scarcely possible to rise higher than this."

Mixing the supernatural and the demonic with representations of peasant life and unsullied Nature, *Der Freischütz* is a primer of Romanticism, and a old-fashioned romance is the dramatic axis of its plot. Max loves Agathe, but cannot marry her until he wins the forest shooting competition. Caspar suggests that he follows his example and sell his soul to the evil spirit Samiel. He tells Max about a set of magic bullets being cast in the Wolf's Glen at midnight, then at the contest he tricks him into shooting at Agathe (whose form is represented by a dove). All ends well: the bullet misses and Caspar is made to pay Samiel's fatal price, because Max did not act of his own free will.

Der Freischütz's quality is clear right from the overture. Using different keys to portray contrasting emotions (C major for good, C minor for evil), it is innovative in being constructed almost entirely from material heard later in the opera, and Weber's deployment of the orchestra is amazingly inventive: accompanied by low clarinets, tremolo strings and off-beat timpani, the mysterious last twelve bars of the overture are the very distillation of German Romanticism. The sense of dramatic cohesion is enhanced through Weber's use of leitmotif. Characters and key ideas are associated with certain motifs, some of them sung, many of them expressed in connection with a particular instrument or harmony. Often these motifs can be found lurking just beneath the melodic surface, creating a substratum on which the action rests – and foreshadowing the massive music-dramas of Wagner.

Weber's melodies are astounding in their number and quality (he was often referred to as the German Bellini), and the choruses, specifically those sung by the hunters and bridesmaids (who arrive mid Act III), are exceptionally rich and buoyant, while the dances, notably the march and waltz of Act I, remain equalled only by the dance music of Johann Strauss the Younger. One episode stands out above all the rest: the depiction of the Wolf's Glen is one of the most engrossing creations in all German opera, and the finest example of musical scene-painting before middle-period Wagner. Mysterious harmonies, monotone choruses, mixed spoken and sung dialogue, and sumptuous, multi-layered orchestration contribute towards a genuinely intimidating evocation of unearthly powers.

Of the many recordings available the finest is still Joseph Keilberth's 1958 performance for EMI. Its superiority rests with Keilberth's urgent conducting and his stellar cast – the like of which has not been seen since. Grümmer's glowing soprano is ideal for the virginal Agathe and Rudolph Schock's generous tenor makes light work of Max's heroic posturing. Wilhelm Kohn enjoys himself as the wicked Caspar and Hermann Prey, Gottlob Frick and Lisa Otto are peerless in the subsidiary roles of the Hermit, Ottokar and Ännchen. The early stereo has been transferred well to CD.

100

Kurt Weill

Die Dreigroschenoper

Erich Schellow (Macheath), Johanna von Kóczián (Polly Peachum), Willy Trenk-Trebitsch (Peachum), Lotte Lenya (Jenny Diver); Arndt Choir; Radio Free Berlin Dance Orchestra; Wilhelm Brückner-Rüggeberg (conductor)

Sony MK42637; 1 CD; full price

It is now difficult to imagine the shock – both of delight and outrage – provoked by the first performance, in 1928, of Kurt Weill's *Die Dreigroschenoper* (Threepenny Opera). Weill's librettists, Berthold Brecht and the under-credited Elisabeth Hauptmann, based their political satire on John Gay's *The Beggar's Opera* (see p.53), a work in which the realities of London's seamier side were played against the pompous conventions of opera, and thronged their cast with prostitutes, pimps, thieves and murderers in a vivid representation of city low-life. Berlin's opera-going audiences were unused to such things, and Weill's cabaret-infused score and mordant text infuriated the National Socialists, who denounced *Die Dreigroschenoper* as the epitome of Jewish/Bolshevist decadence. But the Brownshirts' hooligan tactics (which chiefly entailed the violent interruption of performances) did nothing to dent the opera's popularity and by 1933, only five years after the premiere, it had received its 1000th performance. Of course, the moment the Nazis took power, *Die Dreigroschenoper* and its Jewish composer were promptly banned.

Brecht and Hauptmann stayed pretty close to their eighteenth-century source. Mack the Knife marries Polly, daughter of the underworld leader Peachum. Betrayed by his in-laws and the prostitute Jenny, Mack is arrested and thrown in jail. Helped by Lucy, daughter of the corrupt police chief Tiger Brown, he breaks out but is recaptured. Waiting to hang, Mack is pardoned by Queen Victoria on her coronation.

Just as Brecht and Hauptmann set out to undermine the niceties of Germany's bourgeoisie, so Weill's music aimed at "the complete destruction of the concept of music-drama". Written in verse-song with pauses for spoken dialogue and any necessary action, *Die Dreigroschenoper* is effective primarily because of the way in which Weill wraps the mockery of the text in the sweetest and most insinuating music, so that the words have a sort of delayed action effect. The caustic ironies of *Die Dreigroschenoper* are a world away from the contrapuntal extravagances of Wagner, Strauss and all those composers for whom Evil was a diminished seventh and Good a rising fourth. Weill's style is that of a classicist whose vocabulary has been transformed through contact with popular music into something dry and spiky, and thoroughly well-suited to the world-view of Brecht. Numbers such as the seditious "Ballad of the Good Life" and the gruesomely funny "Don't Prosecute Crime, It Will Die Out of its Own Accord" attest to a rare accord between composer and librettists, as does the libidinous "Ballad of Sexual Dependency", which so shocked the first Mrs Peachum that she refused to sing it. Best of all, however, is the sexily murderous "Mack the Knife", a slinky number made famous through performances by Louis Armstrong and Frank Sinatra.

For its authentic flair and extraordinary energy Brückner-Rüggeberg's 1958 recording of *The Threepenny Opera* is essential listening. Weill's wife, Lotte Lenya, created the role of Jenny two years after their marriage in 1926, and her wonderfully insidious performance drips with true cabaret style. The music-hall flair of Erich Schellow's Macheath and Willy Trenk-Trebitsch's Peachum fit in nicely, and Wolfgang Neuss – a singing actor – is suitably spooky as the Street Singer, bringing wonderful menace to his performance of "Mack the Knife". The rest of the cast are similarly free of operatic affectation and Wilhelm Brückner-Rüggeberg's conducting is so natural as to make the whole thing sound improvised. Although the sound is very much of its time, this is the real McCoy, and vastly preferable to the largely operatic, if better recorded, alternatives.